Acknowledgement

Anthony Reeves would like to thank Anna for reading
the early drafts and Nigel for giving him an opportunity.
Special thanks to Fiona for all her support.

THE EMPLOYMENT HANDBOOK

A guide for
employers and employees

Anthony Reeves

700026710610

Fitzwarren Publishing

©Fitzwarren Publishing 2003

First published in 1996
Second edition 2003

British Library Cataloging in Publication Data
A CIP record for this book is available from the British Library

ISBN 0-9545934-0-5

Published by:
Fitzwarren Publishing,
2 Orchard Drive, Aston Clinton

Printed in England by Halstan & C

CONTENTS

1. Introduction 1

Main areas covered 1; regulations due to come into force soon 1; employment tribunals and industrial tribunals 2; legal representation 2; The Employment Act 2002 and changes to be implemented 2; the need for work permits 2; statutory rights 2.

2. What is an Employee? 5

Definition of an employee 5; the various tests to determine status 5; the benefits of being an employee 7; obligations upon an employer in respect of employees 7; types of workers 8; agency staff 8; homeworkers 10; company directors 10; ministers of religion 10; partners 10; IR35 11.

3. The Contract of Employment 13

Elements for a contract to come into existence 13; types of contractual terms 14; express terms 14; statement of employment particulars 15; implied terms 17; examples of terms implied into contracts 17; variation of the terms of an employment contract 19; types of employment contracts 20; particular terms of employment contracts and sample clauses 20; example of contract of employment 22.

4. Employment Protection 26

Employees' rights 26; working time regulations 26; working time regulations opt-out 27; paid annual leave 28; rest periods 29; rest breaks 29; night workers 30; references 31; national minimum wage 31; maternity leave and pay 32; parental leave 33; paternity leave and pay 33; time off for family emergencies 34; flexible working regulations 35; part-time workers 35; fixed term contract workers 36; miscellaneous other rights of an employee, including right to be paid, itemised pay statements, unlawful deduction of wages and statutory sick pay 37.

5. Public Interest Disclosure 39
Whistleblowers' charter 39; background to Act 39; types of disclosure which qualify for protection 39; ways of disclosure to secure protection 40; compensation 42; duty of complainant 43.

6. Health & Safety at Work 44
Liability of employers 44; Health & Safety at Work Act 1974 44; Duties of employers 44; safe place of work 45; safe system of work 45; management of health & safety regulations 46; list of the other five regulations in so-called 'six pack' 47;   Manual Handling Operations Regulations 47; Health and Safety (Display Screen Equipment) Regulations 47; Noise at Work Regulations 47; employees' duties 48; basics of a successful health and safety policy 48; formulating a policy 49; implementing a policy 49; measuring and reviewing performance 49; enforcement and the Health & Safety Executive 50; the employer's defence 50.

7. Redundancy and Transfer of Undertakings 51
Definition of redundancy 51; situations in which redundancy may arise 52; reasons you may not be able to claim redundancy 53; offers of alternative employment 54; procedure 55; transfer of undertakings legislation 57; compensation for redundancy 58.

8. Termination of Contract & Wrongful Dismissal 59
Classification of termination 59; operation of law 59; frustration 60; agreement of both parties 60; dismissal 60; remedy for wrongful dismissal 61; damages 61.

9. Unfair Dismissal 63
Do you have a claim 63; was your dismissal fair 64; automatically unfair dismissals 64; potentially fair reasons for dismissal 65; capability 66; qualifications 67; conduct 68; conduct outside employment 68; disciplinary and grievance procedures 69; The ACAS Cose 69; Employment Act 2002 70; summary of minimum dismissal and disciplinary procedures

70; standard grievance procedure 71; redundancy 72; statutory restriction 72; remedies for unfair dismissal 73; calculation of compensation 73; compensatory award 74; additional award 74.

10. Restraint of Trade Clauses 75

Restrictive covenants 75; most common clauses 75; unreasonable restrictive covenants 77; reasonable clauses 80; enforcing a restraint clause 81.

11. Discrimination 82

Types of discrimination 82; main legislation covering discrimination law 82; direct discrimination 82; indirect discrimination 83; job advertisements 84; interviews 84; sexual harassment 85; race discrimination 86; indirect race discrimination 86; victimisation 87; vicarious liability 87; disability discrimination 88; defences to discrimination 90; remedies 90.

12. Making a claim to an industrial tribunal 91

Time limit 91; the employment tribunal 91; beginning proceedings 92; responding to a claim 96; ACAS settlement 97; compromise agreements 98; interim applications 100; questionnaires 101; Form SD74 101; the bundle of documents 104; witness statements 104; the hearing 105; the decision 106; an appeal 107.

13. Trade Unions & Industrial Action 108

What is a trade union 108; independence and recognition of trade unions 108; closed shops 109; industrial action 110; statutory immunities 110; what is a trade dispute 111; secret ballots 112; official or unofficial action 112; picketing 114; employer's remedies against employees 114.

Specimen forms 116

Application to an Employment Tribunal 116; Notice of Appearance by respondent 118.

1

INTRODUCTION

Employment law is a rapidly developing area, becoming more complicated as each new piece of legislation is introduced. As it is such a vast subject, it is beyond the scope of this book to cover every aspect of employment law but the most important areas have been selected for explanation in straightforward and jargon-free language.

Some of the main areas covered - such as unfair dismissal - form the majority of claims brought before an employment tribunal. Although this book is primarily of interest to employees seeking initial guidance on employment rights, it will also prove a useful reference guide to professionals, such as personnel managers and small businesses faced with a legal employment problem. Indeed, employers can avoid many legal pitfalls by acquiring a basic understanding of the relevant laws and regulations and by considering at an early stage the issues involved.

Readers of any legal handbook should bear in mind the ever-present problem for publishers and authors of new legislation being proposed or introduced at the time of publication. With a book on the rapidly changing subject of employment law such a problem is especially relevant. A line has to be drawn at some stage but we briefly mention in this chapter some important reforms not mentioned elsewhere which are expected to become law in the near future.

Not only is domestic legislation bringing forward new employment law, but Directives from the European Union have also created a vast number of new regulations. A whole host of proposed regulations prompted by new European Directives are in the pipeline.

From December 2003, a number of Regulations implementing Directives will become law in the UK. At the moment, employers have a duty not to discriminate on grounds of race, sex or disability but from December 2003, the Equal Treatment Directive of 2000 will come into effect also outlawing discrimination in the work place on the grounds of

1

sexual orientation and religion. Looking further ahead, there are changes due to be implemented in the areas of noise, disability discrimination and new regulations to outlaw age discrimination. The changes to the noise regulations will reduce the level of permitted noise in the workplace. Disability legislation is set for some important changes with exemption for businesses with less than 15 employees to be removed.

The likely timetable for the introduction of these new regulations is:

Disability Discrimination Amendments - October 2004
Age Discriminations Regulations - October 2006
Health & Safety at Work/Noise -November 2005

When an employee believes that an employer has breached one of his rights, such as the right not to be unfairly dismissed, then the employee may make a complaint to an Employment Tribunal. Employment Tribunals were previously known as 'Industrial Tribunals' and were introduced in 1964, changing their name in 1998.

These tribunals were originally intended to have little involvement from lawyers but this has not proved to be the case. Although legal aid is not available and rarely will a costs order be made against a losing party, many employees have obtained funding and representation through a trade union or bodies such as the Equal Opportunities Commission in cases of discrimination.

Despite the relatively informal setting of tribunals, which would favour employees representing themselves, figures suggest that employ- ees who have legal representation at an employment tribunal have a greater chance of succeeding. There have been concerns about the increased number and complexity of cases being dealt with by employ- ment tribunals.

New powers that allow tribunals to streamline the handling of cases and to award costs against individuals who waste the tribunals' time will be introduced as part of The Employment Act 2002, which will gradual- ly come into effect from 2003.

The Employment Act 2002, a very significant piece of legislation, is largely an enabling statute which provides powers to introduce new Regulations in various areas. Some of the main changes implemented by the Employment Act 2002 are as follows:

April 2003:
Six months' paid and a further six months' unpaid maternity leave
Two weeks' paid paternity leave for working fathers
Six months' paid leave and a further six months' unpaid leave for adoptive parents
An increase in the rate of maternity pay to £100 per week

April 2004
Changes in the way tribunals calculate awards to encourage dispute resolution
Fast track systems and other measures to modernise employment tribunals

October 2004
New ways of handling disputes in the workplace and requirements for employees to raise grievances with their employer before applying to a tribunal

When recruiting employees, employers should ensure that they comply with various legal requirements. An employer has an obligation to ensure the employee is legally entitled to work in this country.

Citizens of the European Union and the European Economic Area do not need work permits and they have the right to come to the UK and look for work. If an individual is subject to immigration controls then a work permit must be obtained unless the employee is within one of the exempt categories.

On entering into a contract of employment, an employee becomes entitled to statutory rights. This book is unable to cover every single employee right but concentrates on some of the more important areas such as Minimum Wage, Working Time Regulations, Public Interest Disclosure, Redundancy, Unfair Dismissal and Discrimination.

With the incredible amount of new employment legislation being introduced, the subject is becoming somewhat of a minefield with even lawyers finding it difficult to keep abreast of developments. This book is not intended to be a comprehensive statement of employment law.

Readers should bear in mind that a 'little knowledge is a dangerous thing' and in attempting to simplify the subject in a useful handbook of this size it may be that some minor details which have been omitted are vital in answering your particular legal question.

Every effort has been made to ensure that the information is a correct statement of the law at this time but as the law in this area is so rapidly changing, some aspects of this book may be out of date by the time you read them. It is therefore recommended that anyone with a specific legal problem should take independent legal advice.

Neither the author or the publisher can be held liable for losses arising from reliance on information contained herein.

- Anthony Reeves
September 2003

2

WHAT IS AN EMPLOYEE?

The status of a worker has great legal significance. In many situations the answer may appear obvious but this question is not always clear and has created considerable legal discussion. The distinction between an employee and a self employed person is important because the legal rights of each are different. An employee is entitled to greater statutory and common law protection than a self employed person.

The distinction involves some difficult points of law.

Definition of an employee

The general statutory definition of an "employee" for the purposes of employment law is an individual who has entered into or works under a 'contract of employment' (or 'contract of service'). Only individuals within this definition have many of the rights - such as unfair dismissal and redundancy pay - provided under the Employment Rights Act 1996,

A person who works under a 'contract of employment' is different from a self employed or independent contractor who works under a 'contract for services'. Whether an individual is an employee is also of importance for other purposes, such as income tax, social security, and the liability of employers to third parties for the wrongful acts of their employees.

What a worker is called is not the decisive factor in determining whether or not he/she is an employee. Courts consider the true nature of the relationship between the parties. Several tests have been developed by the courts to determine the status of a worker, including:

· The Control Test
· Mutual Obligations Test
· Organisation Test
· Multiple Test

Under the control test, an individual is regarded as an employee where the employer not only controls when the job is done, but also how it is

5

done. This test operates well with unskilled workers but falls down with more skilled workers who decide how their work should be done.

Mutual obligations is a strong indicator that a worker is an employee; the test is whether an 'employer' is obliged to provide work and whether the worker is obliged to perform work for the 'employer'.

Under the organisation test, a person who is an employee is integrated into the business, whereas an independent contractor is not.

Over the years, the courts have decided that no one factor decides the nature of the employment relationship. The courts look at all the factors and make a balanced decision.

Therefore, the predominant test currently used is the 'multiple test'. This test began in the case of Ready Mixed Concrete (South East) Ltd v. MPNI (1968), where the question was whether a group of lorry drivers were employees or independent contractors. Judges balance a host of factors to reach a decision on the worker's employment status in the multiple test. Some of the factors which the court will consider in a multiple test include:

> *Does the person work under the orders or regular control of another*
> *Does the person work exclusively for the other party*
> *Does the person work as part of the other's business*
> *Does the person provide their own equipment*
> *Does the person provide their own support staff*
> *Who is responsible for the payment of Tax and National Insurance*

It is important to balance all the factors of a particular case. If you consider factors in isolation you may reach a possibily incorrect and different conclusion to that which you might have reached had you judged all the factors together.

For example, suppose a tool maker pays his own income tax and national insurance. That on its own might indicate self-employment, but if you also consider the fact that he works exclusively for one engineering company and uses their tools and equipment, then he is more likely to be regarded as an employee.

To further illustrate how the multiple test is applied, consider the following case of Sophie and Collections Ltd. Is she self employed or an employee?

Sophie is a credit controller for Collections Ltd. She works three days a week and has done so for six years. When at the office, she uses the company's computer equipment. She works for nobody else and is subject to the day-to-day direction and control of the Finance Director.
Due to the installation of a new computer system, Collection Ltd wishes to dispense with her services. They regard her as self employed and give her one week's notice.

In applying the multiple test, Sophie is a part-time employee. The important factors that support this view are that she uses the company's equipment, works exclusively for Collections Ltd and is subject to the direction and control of the finance director. She would be entitled to statutory notice, redundancy pay and may be able to challenge the dismissal if it was unfair.

There are major benefits of being an employee. Among them are :
- protection against unfair dismissal (assuming sufficient continuous employment - see Chapter 9)
- redundancy pay
- notice of termination of employment
- written particulars of employment
- equal pay
- maternity rights
- national minimum wage
- paid annual leave
- limitation on working time
- parental leave

The employment status of a worker will also affect the employer. The term 'employer' is not defined by statute. The term acquires significance when deciding who is responsible for the negligence of another person. Employers are liable for the civil wrongs committed by their employees in the course of their employment

There are also a whole host of other obligations on an employer in respect of their employees, such as insurance, PAYE and health and safety.

Types of Workers

Labels in employment law can be misleading and do not always assist in deciding whether or not a person is an employee. There are various types of workers where this may be the case:

Agency staff:

These workers, often referred to as 'temps', are sent by an employment agency to work for a separate organization. For these workers there are normally two contracts. One is between the worker and the agent and another between the agent and the direct recipient of their services (usually the company where the temp has been sent by the agency).

In most of these arrangements, the agency places the worker and pays the worker direct. The problem is often the relationship between the worker and the recipient company.

Over a period of time, it is possible for the relationship to develop into a contract of employment. The following case study concerning Mrs Black considers the point of whether a temp is employed by the agency or the company where the temp is conducting the assignment.

Mrs Black and The Employment Agency

Mrs Black went to Smiths Temp Agency looking for part time work. The agency found her a position as a receptionist/typist at Bloggs Engineering. After agreeing the hours of work and rates of pay, Smiths wrote to Mrs Black to confirm the position and set out its terms and conditions. The agency paid her for the hours she worked accordingly to time sheets agreed by the company, payment going directly into her bank account. Mrs Black was under the supervision of Mrs Stern, the Admin Manager at Bloggs Engineering. Mrs Stern would tell Mrs Black whether she wanted her to do more typing and less reception work when there was a backlog in the secretarial section.

Two years later, the company became dissatisfied with Mrs Black's work and asked the agency to terminate the assignment. Mrs Black wants to make a claim for unfair dismissal but is she an employee of the agency or Bloggs Engineering?

In this situation, Mrs Black would almost certainly be regarded as an employee of Bloggs Engineering. Although an assignment organised by the employment agency might in certain circumstances establish sufficient control to make them the employer, in this particular case the agency had little or no control, direction or supervision of the worker. Mrs Black was under the direction and supervision of Mrs Stern of Bloggs Engineering. She was therefore an employee of the company and not the agency.

There are situations where the law will regard an agency worker as an employee of the employment agency in respect of assignments, despite the wording of the contract signed with the agency. The status of a worker supplied by an employment agency to a third party on a temporary basis has to be determined by reference to all the terms of the contract and the facts of the case. Even if the contract with the employment agency describes the worker as self employed, the facts of the assignment could indicate that the worker is in fact an employee of the agency. If it is clear that the worker is not in business on his/her own and the agency exercises considerable control over the worker, then that worker is an employee of the agency.

There are other cases where agency workers are regarded as temporary employees of the recipient company for the duration of the work assignment. An example of this is where employment agencies supply temporary drivers to transport companies.

In the case of Interlink Express Parcels Ltd v. Night Trunkers Ltd & Another (March 2001) the Court of Appeal decided that the drivers who were supplied by Night Trunkers were temporarily deemed servants [employees] of Interlink. Although Night Trunkers paid the drivers, the court said that in this context it should apply the control test. Interlink controlled the drivers in that they specified the required qualifications, directed the routes, instructed the drivers on cleaning the vehicles, time sheet completion and the servicing of vehicles.

It should be mentioned that in this case, had the drivers been found to be employees of the agency and not the transport company, then the agency would have been in breach of transport regulations as they did not have an operators licence.

The status of agency workers is made more confusing because under legislation, agency workers are defined as 'employees' for the purpose of statutory paid annual leave, statutory minimum wage, rest breaks, and limits on the average weekly working time.

The Working Time Regulations 1998 specifically provide that agency staff who would not otherwise be covered by the Regulations because of an absence of a contract with the agent or principal, are taken to be employed by whoever is paying them.

Homeworkers:

As the name suggests, these workers undertake their work in their own home or away from the premises of the other party. Again, the courts look at the true nature of the relationship between the parties. Where a regular pattern of work is provided these workers can be employees

Mary works from home packing greeting cards into boxes for Media Card Ltd. The materials are delivered to her twice a week and the completed work is collected. Mary is paid for each box she packs. Mary is free to choose the amount of hours she does per week, subject to a minimum.

It is likely that Mary will be regarded as an employee and will therefore be entitled to all the statutory protection and benefits.

Company Directors:

The general position is that a company director is an 'office holder' and not an employee. If there is a 'service agreement' which requires a director to perform tasks in return for a regular salary, then the courts will usually regard this agreement as a contract of employment and so regard the director as an employee of the company.

Ministers of Religion

Ministers of Religion are regarded as 'office holders' and so are not employees.

Partners

Partners are not usually employees. They are self-employed, receiving a share in the profits generated by the business. However, a 'salaried partner' does not own a distinct part of the business and receives payment by way of salary only. A salaried partner is generally regarded as an employee.

In the case of Marsh Ferriman & Cheale v. Ms H Cutler (1998) the question was whether a salaried partner in a firm of solicitors was self-employed or an employee for the purposes of claiming unfair dismissal. During her time with the firm Ms. Cutler had authority to write cheques and to send out invoices. Although she was invited to attend partnership meetings she did not have a vote on financial matters.

She was taxed as an employed person, the sums being deducted from her salary by the accountants who did her tax returns. In addition, she was held as a partner on the firm's letterheads and on bank guarantees. She had no share in the firm's profits and had no responsibility for the liability of the firm.

The firm of solicitors appealed against the employment tribunal's decision that Ms Cutler was an employee. The appeal was dismissed. The Court said that to decide if she was an employee, it had to consider whether she performed the services in business on her own account. It decided that the answer was no and so she was an employee.

IR35

The term IR35 stems from the rules first proposed in a 1999 Budget press release numbered IR35. The purpose of the rules was to remove opportunities for the avoidance of income tax and national insurance contributions, by using intermediaries such as service companies.

Until the full introduction of IR35 on 6 April 2001, there were tax and National Insurance advantages in arranging for a customer (who might otherwise be an employer) to make payments to a company owned by an individual who was providing services rather than to the individual.. The 'employer' also benefited from this arrangement as the chances of the individual concerned being regarded as an employee for unfair dismissal and other purposes of the employment protection legislation were reduced because the contract was not clearly an 'employer/employee' contract.

With the growth of consultancy work, especially in the IT industry, the 'one man service company' method of working became more and more popular.

In essence, the law introduced by IR35 addressed the question, for tax purposes, of whether the relationship between two people is one of employer/employee or employer/independent contractor.

A recent case concerned Synaptek Ltd v. Young (Inspector of Taxes) (April 2003) The court had to consider whether or not a software consultant was an employee. The consultant, Mr Stutchbury, was in business on his own account as a software consultant and acquired Synaptek Ltd. He and his wife were the only shareholders and directors. Synaptek Ltd, through an agency, made an agreement with a government department for the provision of Mr Stutchbury's services for a period of six months.

Factors in support of his being an independent contractor included:

▾ *The requirement for Mr Stutchbury to have professional indemnity insurance*

▾ *The limited control by the client of the time and manner in which he performed his services*

▾ *The flexibility of his working hours and the fact that he used his own reference books*

But the factors that indicated he was an employee included:

▾ *The minimum working hours agreed were broadly equivalent to a normal working week*

▾ *He worked alongside the client's employees and was sufficiently integrated with its workforce to have a line manager*

▾ *He agreed to comply with all of the client's instructions*

After weighing up all factors, the court decided that Mr Stutchbury was an employee.

Even before IR35, the courts were developing a similar theme in non-tax situations for the benefit of workers who might otherwise be denied employee rights. Although the distinction between 'employee' and 'self employed' is still extremely important, it is gradually becoming less so for employment law purposes as working patterns change.

There is a move towards extending statutory employment rights to everyone who qualifies as a 'worker' rather than just those who qualify as an 'employee'. The definition of a 'worker' is less restrictive, so it would mean more people receiving statutory rights. This principle is applied in several pieces of legislation including the Working Time Regulations 1998 and the National Minimum Wage Act 1998.

3

THE CONTRACT OF EMPLOYMENT

A contract of employment follows the basic principles of any other contract. With an employment contract, there are certain additional requirements imposed in respect of its form and content. The basic elements for a contract to come into existence are:

▸ *An offer*
▸ *An acceptance*
▸ *Payment or benefit*
▸ *Intention to create legal relations*

An employer must make a clear offer of a job to the employee, who must equally clearly communicate his acceptance to the employer. Finally, the agreement must be for money or some other benefit. The offer and acceptance can be made verbally or in writing.

Therefore, a contract can exist between the employer and employee even if there is no written documentation. Having a written document does make it easier to show what terms were agreed should there be a dispute, and this is something every employee should insist upon

It is usual after a successful interview for an employer to make an offer verbally to the employee. The employee accepts the offer verbally and the employer sends a formal letter of appointment in which he also sets out the main terms and conditions. There will be situations where an employee will not receive a formal offer letter before the start date.

Consider Frank's predicament in the following situation.

Frank goes for an interview on Wednesday at Fastlink Sales Ltd. Sales Director, Sue Fixit interviews him and telephones him on Friday, offering him the job to start the following Thursday. Having worked out notice on his previous job, Frank can start on the day in question.

He turns up for work and is told by Sue that she has changed her mind about the job offer. Sue believes she can do this as nothing has been signed.

13

Fastlink Sales Ltd is in breach of contract. Although no documents were signed, an offer was made orally by Sue, which was accepted by Frank. He is entitled to receive notice of termination of the contract or payment in lieu of notice.

The law states that someone who has been employed for less than a month is entitled to reasonable notice, though that may be less than one week. In Frank's case as he did not actually start the job he may only be entitled to one day's notice. As the amount of payment in lieu of notice is likely to be small it would probably not be worthwhile pursuing it.

The contract of employment gives an employee and employer rights and obligations. The rights an employee has under the contract of employment are in addition to those rights granted by legislation.

Generally, the employee and employer can negotiate whatever terms they want, but they cannot agree terms that give the employee less rights than those granted by legislation. Accordingly, freedom of the parties to agree terms is restricted by various pieces of legislation so that an employer cannot:

▶ Restrict its liability for the death or personal injury of his employees caused by his own negligence

▶ Include terms which infringe certain legislation such as that relating to equal pay, sex discrimination and race relations

▶ Take away an employee's right to bring an action in the courts or employment tribunal unless there is a fixed term contract of two years or more with a properly worded waiver provision

A contract of employment consists of two types of contractual terms - Express terms and·Implied terms

Express terms

Express terms are those that have been specifically agreed between the employer and employee, for example the rate of pay. Such terms would have been agreed orally or in writing.

Express terms are those agreed by the parties. There are certain terms that an employee will want to know before accepting the job, such as the hours of work and the salary. Having express terms is sensible as it ensures certainty with both parties knowing where they stand, provided the terms are not ambiguous.

Badly drafted terms of employment have caused problems for employers. If a term is in dispute then a court will decide its meaning. As the express terms are intended to show the intentions of the employee and employer, if the term is inaccurate then it could lead to problems.

An example of such a problem occurred in the case of Stubbes v. Trower, Still & Keeling (1987). This case concerned a firm of solicitors who offered articles (the old name for a training contract) to a law student but failed to include an express term that the applicant had to pass the Law Society Finals before he could start. To qualify as a solicitor, a law student has to complete a two-year training contract under the supervision of a solicitor. In this case, the Court of Appeal decided that to be required to pass the Law Final Examination was not a requirement of the articles.

Generally, express terms will have priority over implied terms. The following example illustrates this principle.

UK Engineering advertised for a 'sales engineer (export)'.
Robert applied for the job and was given it. The contract of
employment described him as a 'sales engineer'.
He argued that the job was limited to export because of the
advertisement.

In this situation, the courts have decided that the contract takes priority. If the term is clear the express term will not be overridden by an implied term. It is likely that Robert's job would not be limited to export.

Statement of Employment Particulars

Under the Employment Rights Act 1996 there is an obligation upon the employer to provide the employee with written details of the job within two months of starting the employment. If an employer does not supply written details, then an employee should request them.

Ultimately, if the employer fails to provide the required particulars then a complaint can be made to a tribunal which can order that it be given and impose a fine on the employer. The statement must include the following:

- The name of the employer and employee
- The date when the employment began
- The date on which the employee's period of continuous employment began even if it is not different from the date when employment commenced
- Hours of work
- The rate of pay and the interval between payments
- Entitlement to sick pay
- Pension entitlement
- Notice period

The notice period required by the employer to terminate the contract must not be less than the statutory minimum.

Requirements of notice for each period of continous service are as follows:-

Less than one month - a reasonable period of notice

> *One month to 2 years - 1 week*
>
> *2 -12 years - 1 week for each complete year of service;*
>
> *Over 12 years - 12 weeks' notice*

(The employee must give the employer at least one week's notice where he has one month's service or more. Unlike the notice required by employers, this does increase with the length of the employee's service.)

- Job title or job description

The job description should adequately describe the job an employee is required to do. It is lawful for the job description to include broad phrases such as... ' ..and to perform any other duties reasonably within your capability and skills as the interests of the business dictate...'

- Whether the contract is permanent or fixed and if fixed, the date when it is to end
- The place of work
- Any collective agreements where they directly affect the terms and conditions of employment
- Details of employment outside the UK (where relevant)
- Details of disciplinary/grievance procedures

The details of the disciplinary and grievance procedures may refer to an easily accessible separate document such as a staff handbook.

A statement of terms and conditions is not a contract and does not require signature by either party. A contract of employment however usually contains terms in addition to those required by the statutory statement.

Implied Terms

There are two types of implied term; one type considers situations where the contract does not address the dispute in question. In this situation, if the courts are able to interpret the intention of the parties at the time the contract was entered into, then it can imply into the contract the term the parties would have included had they considered the matter in dispute. Effectively, the court 'fills the gaps'. The other type of implied term is where legislation imposes duties into every contract of employment, such as minimum notice requirements.

Over the years, the courts have decided that some terms are important and so must be in every contract. If the parties fail to include those terms in the contract, then they will be implied into the contract. Examples of terms implied into every contract include:

▶ **Duty of trust and confidence**

The law requires every employment relationship to have a duty of mutual trust and confidence. This is another way of saying that there must be respect and co-operation between employer and employee. When one party breaches this duty of trust and co-operation, it is possible for the other party to consider the contract at an end.

▶ **Health and safety**

An employer is under an implied contractual duty to provide employees with a safe working environment. There is also a statutory duty regarding health and safety. Therefore, employees are protected in two ways: by a contractual duty and the health and safety legislation. The employer must also provide safe equipment for use by employees.

▶ **Faithfulness**

This is the implied duty of the employee to work in good faith for the employer and not to engage in work for another business or set up in competition to the employer.

17

▶ Obeying orders

An employee is under an implied duty to obey reasonable and lawful instructions. Failure to do so may legitimately lead to dismissal.

What is a reasonable instruction? An order to perform the duties expressed in the employee's contract will usually be regarded as a reasonable instruction. There will be times when an employee is required to carry out duties that are not within his contract but the instruction is considered reasonable, and other occasions when it is deemed unreasonable to ask an employee to perform certain terms of his contract and where he would not be in breach of contract for refusing.

An example of this would be where an employer orders the employee to work in a particular country whose undemocratic regime has said he would be tortured if he enters the country. Even if the contract required the employee to work in that country, he would be entitled to refuse and not be in breach of contract.

An employee can also refuse to obey an order which is unlawful. So if an employer orders the employee to falsify a set of accounts, then he can refuse and not be in breach of his contract.

▶ Confidentiality

There is an implied duty into every contract of employment that an employee must not disclose confidential information to a third party. Not all information is protected by this implied term. Guidelines have been developed by the courts to help them decide whether or not information is caught by the implied confidentiality term. Courts will consider among other things, whether:

a) the employer has made it clear to the employee that the infomation is to be regarded as confidential
b) the information is easily distinguished from general information
c) a third party may have ways of obtaining the information without being told by the employee

The courts will also consider the nature of the employment, including the status of the employee and the frequency with which they deal with such information.

When drafting a contract of employment, it is important to explain which terms are intended to have contractual force. In addition to contractual terms, the behaviour of employees at work will be governed by rules and procedures, which will change from time to time. These rules and procedures can either form part of the contract of employment or be contained in a separate staff handbook. Staff handbooks should be issued to employees and updated from time to time.

It should be made clear whether or not the staff handbook is intended to be contractually binding. Any rules that are intended to be binding should be a term of the contract. Terms that are in the contract cannot be changed without consent and must be complied with by both sides.

Rules and procedures in a handbook will change over time and so there is an argument for not including them as a term of the contract to allow the employer to change them unilaterally without breaching the contract. If the rules do not have contractual force, the employer can still argue that there has been a breach of the implied duty to obey orders.

Variation of the terms of an employment contract

The general position is that neither employer nor employee can unilaterally alter the terms and conditions of employment, as they can only be changed by mutual consent. Therefore an employer cannot vary a contract simply by giving 'notice to vary'. Such a notice will only have legal effect if it terminates the existing contract and offers a new contract on revised terms.

However, if employees remain at work for a considerable period of time after the revised terms have been imposed, they may be deemed to have accepted the changes. If the worker continues in the post but works 'under protest', then it is a question of fact whether or not the individual has accepted the changes.

Generally, the courts will be reluctant to decide that there has been a variation of the contract by consent if the employee was faced with a choice between dismissal and an alteration in the contract which is against his interests.

In practice, it may be difficult for an employee to resist a variation in his contract. Employers can offer as a fair reason for dismissal the fact that there was a sound business reason for insisting on the changes. Provided there was a minimum amount of consultation and the majority of employees have been prepared to accept the changes, then the employer should be able to convince a tribunal that he acted reasonably in treating a refusal to accept a variation as a reason for dismissal.

Types of Employment Contracts

There are many types of employment contract and .all have their advantages and disadvantages,. But every contract must comply with the employee's statutory rights. Some of the main types of contract include:

▶ Open-Ended Contract
▶ Fixed Term Contract
▶ Short Term Contract
▶ Contracts for Casual Work
▶ Specific Task Contracts
▶ Joint Contracts

Particular terms of employment contracts and sample clauses

The specific wording of an employment contract will depend on the circumstances. However, the following section sets out a sample offer letter and considers some of the main clauses in a contract.

Jackie Chaser and Executive Staff Recruitment
Jackie Chaser sees an advertisement in the Daily Rag for a 'Credit Manager' with Executive Staff Recruitment Ltd. She applies and is invited to an interview with the Managing Director, Nick Bromley, and the Personnel Director Ms Patricia Correctness. The interview goes well and Ms Correctness telephones Jackie the following day to offer her the job. Jackie accepts the offer. Ms Correctness sends out a formal offer letter.

The following is an outline of the type of information that might be included in an offer letter:

24 October 2003

Dear Jackie
Further to your recent interview with Nick Bromley and myself, I write to confirm that we wish to offer you the post of

Credit Manager. It is a short-term contract for 12 months. The offer is subject to satisfactory references.

*1. **Job title and duties:***
Credit Manager- Finance department.:Your duties will include those detailed in the job description dated 10 September, which you received prior to the interview.

*2. **The person to whom you are responsible:** John Brown, Finance Director*

*3. **Normal working hours:** 9.00am to 5.30pm, Monday to Friday*

*4. **Period of Notice:** This is a short-term contract of 12 months duration. If either side wish to terminate the contract in advance of its natural expiry, one month's notice shall be given.*

*5. **Salary:** The salary is £25,000*

*6. **Holiday Entitlement:** 24 days*

*7. **Commencement date:** 6 November 2003*

I would be grateful if you would sign and return the enclosed form to confirm acceptance of the terms set out or referred to in this letter. Please also let me have details of two referees I may approach. One of these should be your current or most recent employer.

I look forward to welcoming you to the company on the 6 November.

Yours sincerely
Ms Patricia Correctness

The following is an extract from Jackie Chaser's contract of employment. The purpose of setting out this extract is to give an illustration of the wording of a contract of employment.

Of course, depending on the actual terms agreed between the parties and the type of employment concerned, the wording may vary and other terms may need to be included. In this particular contract, there are no restraint of trade clauses which in certain contracts would be advisable. Restraint of trade clauses are examined in Chapter 10.

CONTRACT OF EMPLOYMENT

This agreement is made the   day of
XXXX
Between
1.   Executive Staff Recruitment Limited a company registered in England and Wales (registered number XXXXX) of
10 Market Place, Upmarket, Uptonshire ('the Company')
2.   Jackie Chaser of 235 London Road, Upton ('the
Employee')

1.   Commencement of Employment

1.1   The Employee's employment and the Employee's statutory period of continuous employment with the Company will
begin 6 November 2003. No previous employment will count
as continuous employment.

2.   Job Title

2.1 The Employee is employed by the Company as a Credit
Manager. The Employee is responsible to John Brown,
Finance Director.

2.2   It is the intention of both parties that that any description
of the job, duties and responsibilities should act only as a
guide to the major areas for which the Employee is account-
able, unless otherwise specified in writing by the Company.

2.3   Due to the changing nature of the business the Company
reserves the right to change the Employee's job upon providing reasonable notice.

3.   Place of work

3.1   The Employee's initial place of work will be 10 Market
Place, Upmarket.

3.2   The Company reserves the right to change the
Employee's place of work upon giving reasonable notice to
the Employee.

3.3   The Employee will work at such places as the Company
may reasonably require from time to time whether on a temporary or permanent basis, upon reasonable notice being
given by the Company.

3.4   The Employee will travel to such places as the Company may reasonably require from time to time for the proper performance of the Employee's duties.

4.   Duties

4.1   The Employee accepts that the Company may reasonably require the Employee to perform other duties not within the scope of the Employee's normal duties and the Employee agrees to perform those duties as if they were specifically required under this Agreement.

5.   Hours of work

5.1   The normal working hours are from 9.00am to 5.30pm Monday to Friday but the Employee is required to work such hours as are needed for the proper performance of the **Employee's duties.**

5.2   The Employee agrees that the 48 hour week under Regulation 4 of the Working Time Regulations does not apply to the Employee for an indefinite period (subject to the Employee's right to terminate this opt-out agreement on giving three months' written notice to the Company).

6.   Salary and Expenses

6.1   The Company will pay the Employee a salary of £25,000 per annum sterling payable monthly in arrears in equal instalments by bank transfer on or about the last working day of each month.

6.2   The Company shall reimburse the Employee for all reasonable expenses incurred by the Employee in the proper performance of the Employee's duties under this Agreement.

7.   Sick Pay and Absence from Work

7.1   If the Employee is unable to attend work for whatever reason and such absence has not previously been authorised by the Company, the Employee must contact The Personnel Manager by 10am on the first day of the absence to inform the Company of the reason for the Employee's absence.

7.2   If the Employee is absent for period of three working days or more, then the Employee must provide the Personnel Manager with a medical certificate signed by the Employee's doctor.

7.3 If the Employee is absent through sickness or injury the Company will pay the Employee any statutory sick pay to which the Employee may be entitled.

7.4 If the Employee is absent due to illness or injury for a period or periods exceeding three months in any period of twelve months the Company will be entitled to terminate the Employee's employment.

8. Holidays

8.1 The Employee is entitled to 24 days paid holidays exclusive of public holidays, accumulating at a rate of XX days per completed month's employment. Holiday entitlement shall be rounded up or down to the nearest half day.

8.2 The maximum amount of holiday leave that may be taken at any one time is two weeks.

9. Pension

9.1 The Employee is entitled to join the Company's stakeholder pension scheme subject to the deed and rules from time to time in force.

10. Deductions

10.1 The Company reserves the right to deduct from the Employee's salary sums which the Employee may owe to the Company including without limitation, any repayments, loans or losses suffered by the Company as a result of the Employee's negligence or breach of Company rules or policies

11. Confidentiality

The Employee must not at any time during (except in the course of the Employee's duties) or after the Employee's employment, disclose or make use of the Employee's knowledge of any confidential information of the Company. Confidential information includes XXXX

12. Termination of Employment

During the first three months, the notice required by either party to terminate the Employee's employment will be one week. After three months, the notice required by either party to terminate the Employee's employment will be one month.

13. Other Employment

The Employee must devote the whole of the Employee's time, attention and abilities during the Employee's hours of work to the Employee's duties for the Company. The Employee may not, whether directly or indirectly, undertake any other duties for any other interest, business, company or profession during the Employee's hours of work for the Company.

14. Grievance and disciplinary procedures

The disciplinary and grievance procedures apply to the Employee and these are incorporated in the Staff Handbook.

15. Variations to the Employee's terms and conditions of employment

15.1 The Company reserves the right to make reasonable changes to any of the Employee's terms and conditions of employment and will notify the Employee in writing of these changes.

15.2 Such changes will be deemed to have been accepted unless the Employee notifies the Company of any objection in writing within one month of the charge.

16. Law and jurisdiction

This Agreement shall be interpreted, construed and governed by and in accordance with the laws of England and Wales.

4

EMPLOYMENT PROTECTION

In recent years, a wealth of legislation has introduced new rights for employees giving them greater employment protection. It is beyond the scope of this book to examine every employment right but some of the most important, such as those listed below, are considered here:

·*Working Time Regulations*
·*References*
·*National Minimum Wage*
·*Maternity Leave and Pay*
·*Paternity Leave and Pay*
·*Time Off For Emergencies*
·*Flexible Working*
·*Part Time Workers*
·*Fixed Term Employees*
·*Miscellaneous rights*

Working Time Regulations
Working Time

The Working Time Regulations were introduced to implement The Working Time Directive. Parts of the Directive on the Protection of Young People at Work came into force on 1 October 1998. The Regulations apply to 'workers', which means individuals working under a contract of employment or a contract personally to do or perform work or services, but excluding self-employed people who carry on business activities on their own account.

If a person works through an agency and there is no contract with the agency or the client, then the person responsible for paying the worker is regarded as the employer.

Certain categories of workers - such as police and armed forces - are exempt from the Working Time Directive, but the list of those who are exempt has diminished with recent amendments.

Junior doctors will become covered by the Directive in 2008 at the end of a five year phasing in period.

Those in domestic service will not be covered by the Regulations applying to maximum weekly working time, length of night work and patterns of work.

In occupations where, on account of the specific characteristics of the activity involved, the working time is not measured or predetermined, the maximum weekly working time, length of night work and minimum daily rest periods will not apply. Examples of workers excluded on the basis of unmeasured work are managing executives with autonomous decision making powers, those who work as employees within their own family businesses and workers at religious ceremonies.

What is regarded as 'working time'? The Regulations state that working time means any period during which:

▶ *A worker is working at his employer's disposal and carrying out his activities or duties;*

▶ *Any period during which he is receiving training; and*

▶ *Any additional period that is to be treated as working time under a relevant agreement.*

Time spent on call will not constitute working time, nor will a lunch break spent at leisure as opposed to a working lunch. Travel to and from a place work will not be regarded as working time unless the travel is a required part of the job.

The Regulations state that no worker can work more than an average of 48 hours per week calculated over a 17 week time period. In some situations, the average can be calculated over 6 or 12 months.

A worker may agree in writing that the working time limit does not apply. The worker must be able to withdraw from the opt-out at any time. An example of an opt-out agreement is shown below:

WORKING TIME REGULATIONS 1998 OPT-OUT
BETWEEN:
Sweat Shops Limited   (Employer)
and
Mr A. Work-a-Lot   (Employee)

Restrictions

The Working Time Regulations 1998 provide that an Employee shall not work more than an average of 48 hours each week over a 17 week period unless he agrees in writing that this limit should not apply.

Consent

The Employee hereby agrees that the above restriction on working time shall not apply to his contract of employment with the Employer.

Withdrawal of consent

The Employee may end this agreement by giving the Employer one month's notice in writing.

For the avoidance of doubt, any notice bringing this Agreement to an end shall not be construed as termination by the Employee of his contract of employment with the Employer.

Upon the expiry of the notice period the restriction on working time shall apply with immediate   effect.

Signed: .... (Employee) Dated

At the time of writing, the European Commission is preparing a report to review the opt-out provision, which was a temporary deal negotiated by the UK Government. The European Union may decide that the opt-out provision will have to be abolished because it means the Directive has not been implemented properly.

It has been suggested that the UK Government will try and persuade the European Union to allow the opt-out to continue by increasing the minimum amount of paid holiday.

Since the introduction of the Regulations in 1998, it is estimated that three million British workers have signed an opt-out agreement and regularly work longer than 48 hours a week.

Paid Annual Leave

A worker is entitled to a minimum of four weeks' paid holiday in any leave year.

Neither the European Directive nor the UK regulations which were produced to implement it, refer to Bank or Public Holidays. The right to take Bank and Public Holidays therefore continues to be a matter of agreement between employer and employee. The considered legal view is that if a worker is paid during Bank or Public Holidays those days will count towards annual leave. However it would be an unpopular employer who seeks to enforce it.

The beginning of the 'leave year' will usually be stated in the worker's contract. If it is not expressly stated, then the leave year will start on the date employment began. If employment began before 1 October 1998, the leave year begins on 1 October.

Workers are entitled to receive one-twelfth of the minimum paid leave for each month of service. If employment terminates during a leave year, the employer must make good any annual leave owed by giving payment in lieu.

If the contract of employment allows, and if notice is given which is at least twice as long as the number of days' leave to be taken, an employer may require that all or part of an employee's leave is taken on particular days.. Similarly, an employee must give to an employer notice at least twice as long as the proposed leave to be taken.

Rest periods

A rest period is not working time and it does not include a rest break or leave which a worker is entitled to under the Regulations. An adult is entitled to a rest period of at least 11 consecutive hours in each 24-hour period during which he or she works for the employer. Younger workers, ie those aged 16 or 17, are entitled to 12 hours' rest. In addition, an adult is entitled to 24 hours' rest in any seven day period.

Employers can incorporate all or part of the daily rest entitlement within the weekly period. The weekly reference period can be averaged over a 14-day period. Young workers are entitled to 48 hours' rest in each seven-day period, unless there are organisational reasons to justify a lesser period of 36 hours.

Rest Breaks

Where adult workers work more than six hours a day, they are entitled to a rest break away from their work station. In the absence of any other agreement, the break must be at least 20 minutes long. For young workers, the right to a rest break occurs after 4.5 hours' work and must be at least 30 minutes long. There is no legal requirement that these rest breaks be paid.

Night workers

Night time is a period of at least seven hours duration which includes the period 12 midnight to 5am. The time period is determined by agreement, but in the absence of agreement then the period will be between 11pm and 6am.

An employee is classified as a 'night worker' if they he/she usually works at least threehours of his or her daily working time during this period as a normal course. The normal working hours for a night worker shall not exceed eight hours for each 24 hours.

Normal hours are calculated by reference to a 17 week period.

Arthur and Paper Products

Arthur is a sales executive for Paper Products, a company which produces high quality stationery. Arthur's role is to acquire and maintain customers in the south of England. His area is extensive, covering anywhere south of Watford.

He is required to make regular visits to existing clients and potential clients and therefore he works very long hours, travelling considerable distances each day in the course of his work. Since starting his job with Paper Products, Arthur's family life has changed and he no longer wants to work the 60 hours a week which he has effectively been doing for the past three years.

Arthur speaks to his employer who reminds him of a clause in his contract which states that he must be prepared to work the hours required to undertake his duties. Arthur seeks legal advice as to what he can do.

Arthur has a statutory right not to be required to work more than 48 hours a week. The fact that there is a clause in his contract does not override this right. Even if Arthur had signed a proper opt-out agreement, he would still have the right to withdraw his consent to working more than 48 hours a week by giving notice to his employer.

Arthur could make a complaint to an employment tribunal to assert his rights under the Working Time Regulations. The Health and Safety Executive may also take enforcement action in relation to night work, patterns of work and keeping proper records.

References

Obtaining a good reference from your previous employer is often crucial in securing your next job. However, it is not always appreciated that there is no duty upon employers to give any reference at all.

If a refusal to give a reference is based on grounds of race, sex, any disability or trade union activities, then it is possible for the employee to bring a claim under the relevant discrimination legislation.

If an employer decides to provide a reference, then he owes a duty of care to the employee, and can be held liable for negligent misstatement and damages awarded if a loss is incurred as a result. This principle was established in the landmark case of Spring v. Guardian Assurance Plc and Others (1994). In a later case of Harris v. Trustee Savings Bank (2000), the court warned employers that they must not give 'half the story' in a reference where it would create a misleading impression and could result in damage to the employee.

An employer could be faced with a dilemma when asked to provide a reference. If an employer gives a reference for a previous employee he will have to exercise care in what he says or writes. Some firms will refuse to give a reference rather than write a bad one and risk accusations that it only presented half the story.

Other employers take the approach of including a statement which says that the format of the reference is standard company policy and merely confirm the basic facts about the former employee. In doing this, an employer can argue that a bad inference should not necessarily be drawn from such a reference.

National Minimum Wage

The National Minimum Wage Act 1998 which came into force on the 1 April 1999, makes it unlawful for an employer to pay less than the National Minimum Wage as stipulated from time to time.

There are no provisions which entitle employees to annual or other pay reviews or increases. From October 2003, the level of the Minimum Wage rose to:

£4.50 per hour for workers aged 22 and over:

£3.80 per hour for workers 18-21 inclusive:

Agricultural workers are entitled to the higher rates of minimum pay specified under Agricultural Wages Orders.

The wage of a worker is calculated by dividing the total remuneration by the total number of hours worked. Records have to be kept and must be capable of being produced in a single document at the request of the worker or enforcement agency. The records must be kept for three years.

Workers aged 16 and 17 are excluded from the 1998 Regulations, as are voluntary workers, but the legislation does includes home workers.

Maternity Leave and Pay

All female employees are entitled to a minimum of 26 weeks' Ordinary Maternity Leave regardless of how long they have worked for an employer. Female employees with 26 weeks' continuous employment are entitled to a period of Additional Maternity Leave which runs from the end of the period of Ordinary Maternity Leave.

To qualify for Statutory Maternity Pay, the employee must satisfy the following. She must have:

▾ *worked continuously for 26 weeks or more. The period being calculated as ending in the 15th week before the expected week of childbirth (She could still qualify if the birth is premature)*

▾ *stopped work due to pregnancy*

▾ *weekly earnings not below the current rate for which national insurance contributions must be paid.*

▾ *stopped work no earlier than the 11th week before the expected week of birth unless she gives birth before the start of the eleven week period*

Statutory maternity pay is paid from the date the employee goes on Ordinary Maternity Leave. This must be no earlier than the 11th week - and no later than one week - before the baby is due.

The employee must give her employer 28 days' notice. If 28 days' notice cannot be given, then it should be given as soon as possible. The employer is entitled to ask for a medical certificate to prove pregnancy and the date the birth is due. The employee is paid two different rates of Statutory Maternity Pay during Ordinary Maternity Leave:

▶ For the first six weeks of leave, the employee is entitled to 90% of their her normal pay

▶ After the first six weeks of leave the employee is entitled to a minimum of £100 per week for the rest of the Ordinary Maternity Leave. (If the £100 payment is greater than the employee's weekly wage, the employee will receive her normal weekly pay.)

Statutory Maternity Pay should be paid at the same time as the employee would normally receive payment of wages, for example, weekly or monthly. If an employee is not entitled to Statutory Maternity Pay but has a National Insurance record, she will qualify for 26 weeks' Maternity Allowance at £100 for an employee or a lower amount for the self employed.

If the employee has a contractual right to Maternity Pay, the employer must pay the amount which is the greater.

Parental Leave

Parental leave is in addition to Maternity Leave. The employee must have one year's continuous service and responsibility for a child. The legislation provides for up to four weeks' unpaid leave per year while a child is under five years old, up to a maximum of 13 weeks per child. The employee must give at least 21 days' notice but the employer can postpone the leave for up to six months.

Paternity Leave and Pay

Under the Employment Act 2002, fathers (natural or adoptive) are entitled to two weeks' paid paternity leave if they meet the following conditions. They must:

▶ *have or expect to have responsibility for the child's upbringing*

▶ *be the biological father of the child, the mother's husband or partner*

▶ *have worked continuously for their employer for 26 weeks ending with the 15th week before the baby is due.*

The entitlement is to take one week or two consecutive weeks at any time up to eight weeks from the date of birth or placement for adoption. The employee must give the employer at least 15 weeks' notice before the expected date of the child's birth.

This new right to paid paternity leave is in addition to the 13 unpaid weeks' parental leave entitlement. The leave will be paid at the same rate as Statutory Maternity Pay, £100 per week (or 90% of the employee's average weekly earnings if this is less).

An employer is entitled to reclaim Paternity Pay from the government.

Time Off for Family Emergencies

An employee has a right to take a reasonable amount of time off work to deal with family emergencies. This is unpaid leave and there is no minimum service requirement. The legislation is intended to cover many situations including:

▸ *to provide assistance or make arrangements for the provision of care if a dependant falls ill, is injured or assaulted or gives birth*

▸ *dealing with the consequences of the death of a dependant*

▸ *dealing with the consequences of a child being involved in an incident at school*

▸ *where child care or other arrangements for the care of a dependant break down.*

Under this legislation, the meaning of 'dependant' is a spouse, child, parent or other person living in the employee's household as part of the family.

The employee must tell the employer the reason for his/her absence and how long he/she expects to be absent. An employee can complain to an employment tribunal in cases where the employer refuses time off.

Employees have a right not to suffer a detriment because of time off for family emergencies and any dismissal for this reason is automatically unfair.

The length of continuous service is not a factor in a right to time off for family emergencies.

Sue and Caring & Co

Sue is a single mother who has worked as a secretary and receptionist at a firm of accountants for the past two months. She receives a call from the head teacher of her son's school. She is told that her son Johnny has been caught supplying drugs to younger pupils. The school believes the substance could be cocaine and demands that Sue goes to the school immediately to discuss her son's suspension from school pending an investigation by the police.

Sue's employer is reluctant to allow Sue to leave the office and attend the school but eventually permits her to leave the office for an hour. However she is absent from work for four hours. The next week Sue is given two weeks' notice of termination as her employer says that because they are a a small company they require a secretary who is more reliable.

Sue would be able to make a claim to an employment tribunal as it appears the reason for her dismissal is related to her taking time off for family emergencies, a reason which is automatically unfair.

Flexible Working Regulations 2002

From April 2003, parents and others (such as guardians) who are responsible for looking after children aged under six years old (or under 18 if the child is disabled) acquired the legal right to expect any request they make for flexible working arrangements to be taken seriously.

Such arrangements may be part time working or working from home. The request must be to enable the employee to care for the child and the employee must have been employed in the job for at least six months.

Part-Time Workers

The Part-Time Workers (Prevention of Less Favourable Treatment) Regulations came into force in July 2000. The Regulations make it unlawful for employers to treat part-time workers less favourably than full-time workers. The effect of these Regulations is that part-timers should:

▸ receive the same rate of pay as full-timers

35

▶ receive the same hourly rate for overtime once they have worked more than the normal full-time hours

▶ not be excluded from training.

▶ have the same entitlement to maternity/paternity leave and annual leave on a pro-rata basis

▶ have the same entitlement to pensions

▶ be entitled to written reasons for any treatment which they regard as less favourable and the employer must respond with a written statement within 21 days

These Regulations apply to all workers and all businesses, including small businesses. There will be occasions when the less favourable treatment of part-timers can be justified if it can be shown that it is necessary and appropriate to achieve a legitimate business objective.

As statistics show that most part-time workers are women, employers should consider that if they treat a part-timer less favourably than a full-time employee, they could also face a claim for sex discrimination.

Fixed term contract workers

Regulations were introducedtion in October 2002 which outlawed the less favourable treatment of fixed term workers. Fixed terms workers are those on contracts which either last for a specific period of time, end when a specified task has been completed or when a specified event does or does not happen.

Fixed term workers are entitled to:

▶ not be treated less favourably than comparable permanent employees

▶ receive a written statement from their employer setting out the reasons for any less favourable treatment

▶ treat their contract as a permanent contract if it is renewed for more than four years

▶ qualify for statutory redundancy payment if employed for more than two years

▶ receive information on permanent vacancies within the organisation

▶ claim unfair dismissal for those on 'task contracts' as well as specified period contracts at the end of the fixed term contract if the contract is not renewed and to receive a written statement from their employer with reasons for dismissal

Miscellaneous Rights of an Employee
Right to be paid
The main duty of an employer is to pay his employees. If there is a failure to do so promptly, or at all, the employee is entitled to terminate the contract of employment.

However, the employee must complete what he is contracted to do before he is entitled to claim wages. If an employee has not been paid, he may sue in a county court or apply to an employment tribunal alleging breach of contract.

Itemised Pay Statement
Under section 8 of the Employment Rights Act 1996, every employee is entitled to an itemised pay statement. The pay statement must indicate:
▸ *the gross amount of wages or salary*
▸ *the net amount payable*
▸ *any variable or fixed deductions*

There is no general right to be paid in a particular way.

Unlawful Deduction from Wages
Under section 13 of the Employment Rights Act 1996, it is unlawful for an employer to make any deduction from the wage of an employee unless it is required by statutory provision (for example tax and national contributions), by a provision in the contract or the employee has previously agreed in writing to the making of the deduction.

There are some situations where the provisions will not apply, such as where there has been an overpayment of wages or where a court orders a deduction.

Statutory Sick Pay
Statutory Sick pay was introduced in 1982. An employee is entitled to a weekly rate of £63.25 for the first 28 weeks of illness. After this period, the employee may be entitled to incapacity benefit.

An employee cannot claim for the first three days of sickness and some categories of employees, such as those whose earnings are very low and below the National Insurance threshold, are not entitled to Statutory Sick Pay.

5

PUBLIC INTEREST DISCLOSURE

The Public Interest Disclosure Act 1998, often referred to as the 'whistleblowers charter', came into effect in July 1999. The Act introduced protection for workers who in certain circumstances disclose the wrongdoings of their employers to third parties.

The Act aims to promote better relations between employers and employees over wrongdoings in the workplace and to remove the fear of dismissal or victimisation for those exposing health and safety issues or criminal activities.

The background to the Act lies in the many disasters that happened in the decade before its introduction. Almost every public inquiry into a major disaster found that workers had been aware of the danger but had been too frightened to raise their concerns. The Hidden Inquiry into the Clapham Rail crash heard that an inspector had seen the loose wiring but had said nothing because he did not want to 'rock the boat'. The Cullen Inquiry into the Piper Alpha disaster concluded that workers did not want to put their continued employment in jeopardy through raising a safety issue which might embarrass management.

Under the Act employees are protected from dismissal, selection for redundancy or from suffering any detriment if the reason or principle reason for the action is that the worker has made a 'protected disclosure'.

Certain kinds of disclosure qualify for protection. A disclosure qualifies for protection where the employee reasonably believes that one or more of the following is either happening, has taken place or is likely to take place:

▶ A criminal offence
▶ A failure to comply with a legal obligation
▶ A miscarriage of justice
▶ The health and safety of any individual is in danger
▶ The environment is being damaged
▶ Information relating to any of the above is deliberately being concealed

To understand what the legislation covers, it is important to consider the meaning of some of the above terms. 'Reasonable belief' means that the belief does not have to be correct but only that the worker held that belief and it was reasonable for him to do so.

If a worker, for instance, reasonably but mistakenly believed that a specified malpractice was occurring it would be a qualifying disclosure. If some malpractice was occurring which did not involve a breach of a legal obligation, the disclosure would still qualify if the worker reasonably believed that the situation was a breach of a legal obligation. Unsubstantiated rumours will not be considered a qualifying disclosure as there must be some information which tends to show the particular malpractice.

The six categories mentioned are likely to have considerable overlap. A failure to comply with a legal obligation would include a breach of statutory duty. A miscarriage of justice would cover matters that are likely to cause a wrongful conviction, such as the failure to disclose evidence to the defence.

There is no protection if the disclosure of information is a crime in itself, such a breach of the Official Secrets Act. However, it would not be a breach of the Official Secrets Act if the issue was raised formally within Whitehall or with the Civil Service Commissioner.

An Employment Tribunal will await the outcome of criminal proceedings if they are pending as a result of a disclosure. Should a worker be acquitted then he/she would be able to claim that the disclosure qualified for protection.

The Public Interest Disclosure Act 1998 uses the term 'worker' rather than 'employee' and gives a definition that is somewhat wider than that of employee. The Act includes those people working under a contract of employment, contractors, agency workers, home workers, and every professional in the NHS. It does not currently cover the genuinely self employed (other than those in the NHS), volunteers, the intelligence services, the army or police officers.

There are a number of ways of disclosing wrongdoings in order for such a disclosure to qualify for protection.

> ▸ A disclosure to the employer, or to the person the worker reasonably believes is responsible for the relevant failure *or*

> ▸ A disclosure made in the course of obtaining legal advice *or*

➤ A disclosure made to the Minister of the Crown (if the worker's employer is appointed by statute by a Minister of the Crown) *or*

➤ A disclosure made in good faith to a prescribed person; (a prescribed person/body includes the Inland Revenue, Health and Safety Executive, Financial Services Authority)

A disclosure made to a person other than the employer or to a pre-scribed person may also qualify as a protected disclosure if the worker making the disclosure:

·makes it in good faith
·reasonably believes it to be true
·does not make a personal gain from the disclosure
·reasonably believes that he would be subject to a detriment if
he makes the disclosure to his employer or if he has previously
made a disclosure of substantially the same information to
the employer or the prescribed person.

If the wrongdoing is of an exceptionally serious nature, then some of the procedures for disclosure may be bypassed provided the disclosure is done in good faith and is not done for personal gain.

Frances and Blue Chip Plc

Frances had been working as a stockbroker at Blue Chip Plc for the past 10 months. One Friday morning she overhears her colleague, Mr Awfully-Welloff saying he is going to pur-chase shares in ABC Ltd for a client. He also mentions that at the weekend he is visiting his brother whom she knows is on the board of TBTO Limited. The following Monday Frances discovers that Mr Awfully-Welloff has purchased shares in TBTO Limited instead of ABC Ltd. She wonders why a sud-den change of mind as ABC Ltd seemed a good buy.
A few weeks later the shares of TBTO rise dramatically when the company announces that it is to be taken over by a com-petitor, HBTO Limited. A significant profit is made on the shares purchased by Mr Awfully-Welloff. Frances suspects insider dealing.

> *She speaks to Mr Loadsofmoney, the Director in overall
> charge of the department in which she and Mr Awfully-
> Welloff work. She tells him she believes there is a possibility
> that illegal trading has taken place and requests the matter
> be investigated. Mr Loadsofmoney listens but asks whether it
> is merely a question of rivalry between her and Mr Awfully-
> Welloff.*
>
> *Frances believes that Mr Loadsofmoney has not taken her
> allegations seriously and decides to inform the Financial
> Services Authority. The FSA mounts an immediate inquiry
> which concludes that there was no impropriety by Mr
> Awfully-Welloff.*
>
> *At the end of the month, an opportunity for promotion arises
> in Frances' department. She applies and believes she is a
> very good candidate because she is top of the fee earning
> table for her section. In addition Mr Loadsofmoney had pre-
> viously told her she should apply for promotion when it
> arose.*
>
> *Frances does not get the promotion and feels she has suffered
> a detriment because of raising her belief of wrongdoing by
> Mr Awfully-Welloff.*

The question here is whether or not Frances reasonably believed that a criminal offence had taken place. There was information which tended to show insider dealing so it was reasonable for Frances to hold that belief. She had initially correctly raised the matter with her Departmental Director. His lack of response led her to make a disclosure to a prescribed person, in this case The Financial Services Authority.

The fact that she has been overlooked for promotion amounts to a detriment. Frances has the basis of a complaint and must make a claim within three months. The length of her employment is irrelevant since there is no requirement for a minimum period of continuous employment.

There is no limit to the amount of compensation that can be claimed. Compensation awards are assessed on what is just and equitable in all the circumstances. The losses for which the complainant may claim include expenses reasonably incurred and the loss of any benefit he/she might otherwise have expected.

The complainant is under a duty to mitigate his loss, which if his contract is terminated includes obtaining or seriously seeking another job. It should be remembered that the tribunal has the power, where is decides the worker has contributed to or caused the detriment, to reduce any award by such sum as it considers just.

6

HEALTH AND SAFETY AT WORK

Numerous regulations designed to protect the health and safety of employees at work have been introduced in recent years. Since it has become such a vast subject, this chapter covers only the main aspects of health and safety law and provides guidance on health and safety management.

Many claims against employers arise from accidents at work. Employers can be liable to employees on the basis of:

▶ *Negligence*

▶ *Breach of a statutory duty, such as those imposed under health and safety regulations*

▶ *A breach of contract, such as a breach of the implied term to provide safe premises and equipment and a safe system of work*

The basis of health and safety law is contained in the Health and Safety at Work Act 1974. This Act sets out the general duties that an employer has towards its employees and members of the public, and the duties employees have towards themselves and fellow workers. The 1974 Act is an enabling Act, which means that it has provisions to allow the implementation of other pieces of legislation such as EC Directives.

The 'Framework Directive' 89/391 was adopted to encourage improvements in health and safety in the field of employment. This Directive along with six other directives, were concerned with harmonising health and safety in the EU. It was implemented by a series of regulations introduced at the start of 1993. These regulations became known as the 'six pack', and have been amended a number of times.

Under the Health and Safety Act 1974, 'it shall be the duty of every employer to ensure, so far as is reasonably practicable, the health, safety and welfare at work of all his employees.' This obligation also means an employer must ensure systems of working are safe as well as the place and environment. An employer must also provide adequate training.

Safe Place of Work

The employer's premises must be in good repair and regularly inspected. A place of work that is normally safe can become temporarily unsafe, for example if oil is spilt on the workshop floor and is not cleaned up promptly or properly.

Spillage Limited and Robert Careless

Robert works for Spillage Limited which manufactures soft drinks. He works in the factory as a production line operative. The contents of the bottles regularly spill onto the factory floor. The factory owner allows the floor to be cleaned only once each day as he believes it distracts workers.
The spillages make the floor very wet and slippery and one day Robert slips on the floor and injures his arm.

Robert has a claim for compensation against Spillage Limited because it failed to provide a safe, well maintained, place of work, and a safe system of working. Since the drink is spilt on many occasions, cleaning the floor only once a day is clearly inadequate, as it should be cleared at the earliest opportunity after it is spilt.

Safe System of Work

The method used to carry out the work must be safe. Clearly taking short cut procedures which may increase output at the expense of health and safety is not a safe system of working. But the duty on employers also covers less obvious situations such as adjusting the workload of an employee who has suffered stress.

The case of Walker v. Northumberland County Council (1995) is a good illustration of such a situation. The employee worked for the Council as an area social worker from 1970 until 1987. As a result of the pressure of his workload, and despite his many warnings to his superiors about the level of stress, he suffered a nervous breakdown in November 1986.

He returned to work in March 1987 on the understanding that his superiors would provide him with the assistance of another social worker to ease his workload. The promised assistance was never forthcoming and in September 1987, the employee had another nervous breakdown

The court held the Council liable for the second nervous breakdown. The court decided that the Council ought to have foreseen that if the employee were exposed to the kind of workload that existed before the first breakdown, there was a risk that he would become ill again. When he returned to work after the first breakdown, the Council had to decide whether they were prepared to continue employing him in spite of the fact that he needed additional help. To continue to employ him with no additional help was unreasonable.

The Management of Health and Safety at Work Regulations

The Management of Health and Safety Regulations was the first of a series of six Directives containing the framework regulations which came into force in 1993. Under these regulations, every employer must make a suitable and sufficient assessment of the health and safety risks of his employees.

There are similar risk assessments required for the self employed. Where five or more people are employed, the employer must record the significant findings of the assessment. The risk assessment requires a detailed knowledge and close inspection of the workplace. The Approved Code of Practice relating to risk assessment states that it should:

▶ *ensure all hazards and resulting risks are addressed*
▶ *address what happens in the workplace*
▶ *ensure all employees and others affected are considered*
▶ *identify workers who might be particularly at risk and*
▶ *take account of existing preventative or precautionary measures*

The Management of Health & Safety at Work Regulations also provide that every employer should give his employees - in a form that is understandable - relevant information on the risks to their health and safety identified by the risk assessment and a note of the preventative and protective measures.

There is also a duty on employers to provide employees with adequate health and safety training. Such training is a fundamental provision of these regulations and it is therefore vital that any induction programme for new recruits addresses health and safety training.

The other five Regulations of the so called 'six pack' are:
▸ Protection and Use of Work Equipment Regulations
▸ Manual Handling Operations Regulations
▸ Workplace (Health, Safety and Welfare) Regulations
▸ Personal Protective Equipment at Work Regulations
▸ Health and Safety (Display Screen Equipment) Regulations

It is beyond the scope of this book to examine all of the various Regulations but it is worth providing an outline of the some of them to illustrate how they affect employers and employees.

The Manual Handling Operations Regulations exist to ensure that injuries sustained through lifting and carrying at the workplace are controlled and the prospect of injury is minimised. These Regulations require a risk assessment and that changes be made if required.

Consideration should be given to the capabilities of the employees and if they are required to handle and move heavy loads they must be trained to do so.

The Health and Safety (Display Screen Equipment) Regulations have an impact on most workplaces since computer screens are commonly on employee's desks. These Regulations are designed to protect the health and safety of those who use computers and other display screen equipment.

The employer must assess the employee's workstation to assess whether there are any risks to health, such as the risk of fatigue. The equipment must be adjustable, glare free, appropriately lit and must be maintained at the correct temperature.

The Noise at Work Regulations were introduced in 1990 and impose duties on employers in respect of noise in the workplace. These Regulations refer to three important levels of noise, known as 'action levels':
·First action level - a daily personal noise exposure of 85 db (A)
·Second action level - a daily personal noise exposure of 90 db (A)
·Peak action level - a level of peak sound pressure of 200 pascals

Where an employee is likely to be exposed to the first action level or peak action level, the employer must undertake a risk assessment and inform employees if ear protection is required. If this is the case the employer must provide adequate ear protection.

If the employee is exposed to the second or the peak action level, then the employer must reduce, as far is reasonably practicable, the employee's exposure to noise. If it is not reasonably practicable to do so, then the employee must be provided with personal ear protectors.

Where there are areas in the workplace where employees are likely to be exposed to the second action level or the peak action level, then it must be marked as a ear protection zone and employees should not enter the zone without wearing ear protection.

Finally, but no less important, is the fact that adequate information and training should be provided to the employee on the hazards of noise and the precautions to be taken.

Employees' Duties

So far, all the discussion has been about the duties imposed on employers but employees also have obligations. All employees, whilst at work, have a duty to:

> ▶ *Take reasonable care for their own health and safety and that of other persons who may be affected by their acts or omissions at work*

> ▶ *Co-operate with their employer in ensuring that requirements or duties imposed on the employer in law are complied with*

If an employee is provided with safety boots to use while operating machinery, for instance but refuses to wear them, an employer would be quite justified in threatening disciplinary action.

An employer is under a duty to not only provide the safety boots but also to ensure that they are worn. It is important for an employee to realise that if they are injured while not wearing the safety boots, then any claim they might have against the employer would be heavily reduced because of contributory negligence.

The basics of a successful health and safety policy

The formulation of a statement on health and safety is the starting point for an employer in its management of health and safety. In fact, employers are required by law to have a written policy on health and safety and the arrangements for carrying out that policy. It must be brought to the attention of the employees. This requirement does not apply where there are fewer than five employees.

The following is only an outline of the general principles of health and safety policy. The individual circumstances of each workplace should be considered to ensure that the health and safety aspects of a business are appropriately addressed.

Formulating a statement on health and policy:

In the first instance the employer must identify the hazards. A hazard is something with the potential to cause harm. Trivial risks can usually be ignored, as can risks arising from routine activities associated with life in general.

Having identified the hazards, the employer should determine the arrangements for carrying out the health and safety policy, including what action is necessary. A timetable and proposals for putting the policy into action should be drawn up.

Implementing the health and safety policy:

Once the policy is formulated its conclusions should be put into practice. Employers should ensure that staff are involved and committed. The implementation of the policy simply means that employers must ensure that staff are competent as regards health and safety.

There are many ways an employer can achieve this, but some of the general principles are:

a) selecting individuals to have a position of responsibility

b) providing health and safety training

c) ensuring co-operation and consultation with staff

d) providing suitable control over employees

Measuring and reviewing health and safety performance:

A successful health and safety policy requires continuous monitoring. Monitoring should have regard to the extent of compliance with health and safety legislation by ensuring that standards are adequate, whether or not stated objectives have been achieved within a given timescale and consideration of incident data to analyse causes and trends.

Enforcement and The Health and Safety Executive

The Health and Safety Executive (HSE) has overall responsibility for enforcing the existing health and safety laws and regulations. The laws and regulations are strictly enforced, with a presumption in favour of the claimant.

An HSE inspector has the power to enter premises with or without a police officer to inspect, examine or investigate. In addition, the HSE inspector is permitted to interview representatives of the employer and employees without interference.

After receiving the inspectors report, the HSE may order an improvement or prohibition notice. In certain circumstances, the HSE may bring criminal proceedings against the employer.

Where the employer is a limited company, the proceedings may be brought against a specific director or officer of the company if the breach was committed with the consent, collusion or neglect of that person. However, proceedings against an officer of a company are rare.

The Employer's defence

A common theme that runs through most health and safety legislation is that all employers are obliged to act under the regulations so far as is reasonably practicable in all the circumstances. Therefore, a defence is available to an employer where he can show that he has done all that was reasonably practicable.

7

REDUNDANCY AND TRANSFER OF UNDERTAKINGS

To an ordinary person, the term 'redundancy' may seem self explanatory. However, as this chapter illustrates, redundancy can be a legal minefield. Some employees have contracts that provide for reasonable severance pay. Less fortunate employees need to know their legal rights when facing redundancy.

Employment law provides some protection from the economic realities of redundancy but the amounts allowed under legislation are relatively small.

The statutory definition of redundancy is contained within section 139(1) of the Employment Relations Act 1996:

> *'An employee shall be taken to be dismissed by reason of redundancy if the dismissal is attributable wholly or mainly to:*
>
> *a) the fact that his employer has ceased, or intends to cease, to carry on the business for which the employee was employed by him or ceased, or intends to cease, to carry on that business in the place where the employee was so employed, or*
> *b) the fact that the requirements of that business for employees to carry out work of a particular kind, or for employees to carry out work of a particular kind in the place where he was so employed, has ceased or diminished or are expected to cease or diminish.*

This is a legalistic definition of redundancy. To decide if there is a redundancy situation, the courts consider two questions:

1. Had the requirements of the employer's business for employees to carry out work of a particular kind ceased or diminished, or were they

51

expected to cease or diminish?

2. Was the dismissal of the employee attributable, wholly or mainly, to this state of affairs?

In simple terms, this means that you are entitled to redundancy pay if through no fault of your own, your job ceases to exist or it changes so fundamentally that it is no longer as you had known it. This situation usually arises in four basic situations:

·All or part of your employer's business closes down

If one factory or office in a group shuts down, employees are deemed to have been made redundant if not given suitable alternative employment elsewhere in the group.

To contest redundancy an employer must prove both the suitability of the offer of alternative employment and unreasonableness of an employee's refusal. (Offers of alternative employment are considered later in this chapter in more detail.)

·The business is moved

If an employee's contract contains a 'job mobility clause' in which an employee agrees to work wherever required, the employer may avoid a redundancy situation by offering the employee work in any location.

This is not always a straightforward matter because courts have used different tests to decide the place of work. However, generally even if an employee has a mobility clause in his/her contract and there is a downturn of work in one particular location in which the employer has always worked, this may constitute redundancy.

On the other hand, if an employer decides to transfer work to another location and have an employee move there rather than declare him redundant, this will be lawful unless the reason for the transfer or the manner of the transfer breached the implied duty of trust and confidence. If there was a breach of the duty trust and confidence, it may constitute unfair dismissal.

·The business is sold or taken over

Although the issue can be complicated, as a general rule where the business is transferred as a going concern there is no redundancy as the contracts of the workforce pass to the new owners along with all the other existing contracts. Yet if only the assets are sold, there is usually a redundancy situation. (See the section later in this chapter on Transfers of Undertakings)

·An employee's work is reduced

Reorganisation and new working practices can lead to a reduction in the number of staff required or do away with the need for the work to be done by a particular employee. This will often mean people being sacked but do they have a claim for unfair dismissal or redundancy?

Reorganisation can only create a redundancy if the actual amount of work to be done by any particular employee is reduced. Merely changing the hours of work is not sufficient.

A leading case in point involved two police clerks who worked from 9.30am to 5.30pm each day. The local police asked them to work two daily split shifts, six days a week, in alternate weeks. The Court of Appeal ruled that the change in hours of work was not due to redundancy but due to a reorganisation in the interests of efficiency. The same work was done as before but at different hours.

You cannot claim redundancy pay if:

▶ you normally work outside Great Britain or are self employed, a partner in a firm, a share fisherman, a merchant seaman, a Crown or public servant, policeman, member of the armed forces or domestic servant working for a close relative

▶ you do not have two years' continuous employment. In certain circumstances, the period of continuous employment is not broken even though the employee appears to change employers. This will be the case where there are associated employers and where the business has been transferred.
If a business has been transferred, the period of employment an employee had at the time of transfer will count towards his/her length of service with the new owner. For this to apply, there usually has to be a transfer of the business as a going concern.

▶ you are under 20 or older than 65 unless an earlier 'normal retiring age' applies to your job

▸ you are on a fixed-term contract of two years or more and you have specifically waived your right to a redundancy payment in writing.

All others employed on a fixed-term contract are covered if they have, in fact, worked for at least two years before the date the contract is due for renewal

▸ you have unreasonably refused suitable employment offered by your employer to follow on within four weeks of your old job ending or, having accepted a four-week trial period in new job, you then unreasonably refuse to carry on with it.

▸ you were dismissed for misconduct or as a result of taking industrial action

Offers of alternative employment:

The burden is on the employer to prove both the suitability of the offer and the unreasonableness of the employee's refusal. Offers do not have to contain all the conditions which are ultimately agreed. The employee needs to be given sufficient information to enable him/her to make a decision such as salary, status, and job description

The suitability of the alternative work must be assessed objectively by comparing the terms on offer with those previously enjoyed. The courts have used a test which considers whether the offer is 'substantially equivalent' to the employee's old job. Offering the same salary may not be sufficient, but short-time employment could be suitable if it is full-time.

The fact that the alternative job is at another location does not necessarily mean that it will be regarded as unsuitable. The job could be at a location which is within reasonable commuting distance. In this respect, the employee's contract would probably have contained a clause that he/she could be expected to work at an office which is a reasonable distance away.

When considering the reasonableness of the refusal to accept an offer, subjective considerations can be taken into account. This means factors that are particular to that individual, such as health and family commitments.

It might be reasonable for an employee to refuse an offer of employment, which although suitable, involved loss of status. On this point consider the following example of Mr Chips:

Mr Chips and Downmarket County Council

Mr Chips was a head teacher in charge of the upper years at Downton Comprehensive School. The County Council decided to merge the school with Marketon Comprehensive to form Downmarket High School.

Mr Chips was offered a job as a supply teacher at the new school, but at his old salary. Mr Chips argued that the demotion in status was sufficient to make the new position unsuitable. Does Mr Chips have a case for redundancy?

Although Mr Chips was offered his old salary, generally in such a situation, the courts have decided that a drop in status is sufficient to make the new position unsuitable. A reduction in salary or earnings potential will usually also make the new position unsuitable.

Procedure

Employers must ensure they follow a proper procedure to avoid redundancy amounting to unfair dismissal. An employer should:

▶ Give as much warning as possible
▶ Consult with trade unions, especially regarding selection procedure
▶ Use a selection procedure which is objective
▶ Ensure the selection procedure is followed
▶ Seek to offer alternative employment

Where there is a proposal to make more than 20 employees redundant, there is a statutory duty to consult with trade unions or the appropriate representatives. An employer should consult in good time, but in any case not less than 90 days before the first dismissal when the employer is planning to dismiss at least 100 employees and not less than 30 days before if there is a proposal to dismiss at least 20 employees.

There is no definite guidance on how an employment tribunal should judge the selection procedure. If there is no procedure, then the overall reasonableness of the selection will be considered. Length of service is only one factor.

In applying the procedure, an employer must make sure that he does not breach any of the statutory provisions relating to discrimination. A procedure such as 'last in first out' can be discriminatory against employees with short service but it still remains an important procedure. There will be situations where the selection procedure will be automatically unfair, such as where the reason for the redundancy was trade union activities or pregnancy.

The Yogurt Company and David Ponting

David Ponting is one of three quality control managers at the Yogurt Company which manufactures yoghurt and other dairy products. The Yoghurt Company experienced a downturn in sales the previous year and decides it has insufficient work for the three quality control managers.

David is in charge of quality control for yoghurts, Christine is responsible for milk products and Brian checks the other dairy products such as cheese. It is proposed that two of the quality control managers be made redundant as the level of production only warrants one manager.

The Yoghurt Company decides to cease production of milk and cheese and concentrate on yoghurt. The procedure to decide who is to be made redundant is a written test on aspects of quality control together with an interview with the Managing Director to say why the employee in question should be retained as the sole quality control manager.

David achieves 70% in the test, Christine 65% and Brian 58%. Out of the three, David joined the company before Christine and Brian. To David's surprise, Brian is kept on as the remaining quality control manager. David and Christine are both offered alternative employment. Christine accepts a part-time position in accounts because she intends to fill her remaining time by lecturing at a nearby college.

David is offered the alternative role of 'Assistant Buyer'. The salary is almost the same as in his role of quality control

*manager. He is told that after 6 months training, he will be
on a higher salary than the quality control manager. David
rejects the offer of alternative employment and claims unfair
dismissal.*

David's claim for unfair dismissal raises a number of issues. He
achieved a higher mark than Brian in the written test and so might say
that the selection procedure was not fair. However, the procedure was
not simply the written test as it also involved an interview with the
Managing Director.

It may be that Brian came across better at the interview and so taking
into account the two stages of the selection procedure, he emerged as the
best candidate of the three. David may argue that as he had been at the
Yoghurt Company longer than Christine and Brian, he should have
retained his role on the basis of 'last in first out'. However, having decided on a selection procedure, the Company must ensure it is carried out
as planned and not altered once in progress.

Another issue which the case raises is whether David unreasonably
refused the offer of alternative employment. He may argue that the alternative employment amounted to a drop in status. However, although the
salary would initially be less, it would rise to a figure higher than that of
the quality control manager.

Although a drop in status irrespective of salary can make the offer
unsuitable, it is debatable whether there is a loss of status and after a
short training period it could in fact be argued that he would have
achieved greater status.

For the above reasons, David is unlikely to have a strong case for
unfair dismissal because a tribunal is likely to decide that overall the
selection procedure was reasonable.

Transfers of Undertakings

The Transfers of Undertakings legislation deals with the protection of
contracts of employment and the employment relationship of employees
who are transferred from one employer to another. This subject involves
complicated concepts and is therefore beyond the scope of this book to
examine the topic in detail.

Before the introduction of legislation, the effect of the transfer of a business under Common Law was to terminate the contract of employment.

Under the Transfer of Undertakings (Protection of Employment) Regulations 1981, all contracts of employment automatically transfer to the new organisation on the same conditions as were previously enjoyed by the employees. An employee can object to his/her contract being transferred, but the effect of this would be to terminate the contract without dismissal.

If the proposed transfer would result is a significant and detrimental change to the employee, the employee may terminate the contract and claim unfair dismissal on the basis of constructive dismissal. The 1981 Regulations have been amended by European Directives and further changes are being proposed.

Compensation for Redundancy

- ▶ For each year worked over the age of 18 but under 22, half a week's gross pay
- ▶ For each year worked over the age of 22 but under the age of 41, a week's gross pay
- ▶ For each year worked over the age of 41, but under the normal retirement age, one and a half week's gross pay

A maximum of 20 years can be taken into account when calculating redundancy compensation. There is a statutory maximum 'week's pay', which currently stands at £260. The maximum amount of compensation for redundancy, therefore, is: 20 x 260 x 1.5 = £7,800.

8

TERMINATION OF CONTRACT
AND WRONGFUL DISMISSAL

Wrongful dismissal is often confused with unfair dismissal but the two are not the same. Claims of wrongful dismissal are brought by an employee where an employer has acted in breach of contract because of the way the employment was terminated.

This may be where an employer has ended the contract by giving insufficient notice or no notice at all. It should be remembered, however, that there are situations which justify terminating the contract without notice, such as an employee's gross misconduct.

The termination of a contract of employment can be classified as follows:

▶ Operation of law
▶ Agreement between the parties
▶ Dismissal

Operation of law

The ending of a contract by operation of law includes death, dissolution of a partnership, appointment of a receiver, making a winding up order and frustration.

The death of either employer or employee terminates the contract of employment, but a company itself does not die. Unless there is an express agreement or implied provision, the dissolution of a partnership (for example by death of a partner) will cause the contract of employment to be discharged wherever there is a personal element involved.

An order for compulsory winding-up of a company operates as a notice of dismissal and terminates the contract of employment. Voluntary winding-up and appointment of a receiver may have also this effect. However, this is a complex area and beyond the scope of this book, but much depends on whether the business is to be carried on in some form or another after the winding-up.

Frustration

Frustration will terminate a contract in the following situations:

▸ Where there has been a change of circumstances such that the performance of the contract has become unlawful, for example the passing of a statute after the contract of employment has been made

▸ Where events make it physically impossible for the contract to be performed, e.g. long illness of the employee or imprisonment

The effect of frustration is to end the contract automatically and therefore neither side is liable for damages and an employer is not obliged to give notice.

Many employers dismiss with notice employees who are ill and sometimes this will amount to unfair dismissal..

In long term contracts, it is necessary to view the absence in the context of the whole contract, so for example an absence of five months through illness after two years' satisfactory service may not frustrate a five year contract. There is a difficulty though in knowing where to draw the line.

Agreement of the parties

Contracts of employment can be discharged by agreement.

If a contract is ended by mutual consent, there has been no dismissal and so an employee cannot claim. This can sometimes be of benefit to an employee, as certain clauses restraining their activities after leaving employment may no longer be binding.

The coming to an end of a fixed term contract counts as dismissal for unfair dismissal and redundancy purposes. Whether a particular dismissal is unfair and/or is by reason of redundancy must then be decided according to the normal rules.

Dismissal

There have been few reported claims for wrongful dismissal in recent years, mainly due to the right to claim unfair dismissal. However, there are still situations where a worker may sue for wrongful dismissal, such as where he does not have sufficient continuous service.

A successful claim for wrongful dismissal will have the effect that an employee is discharged from all contractual obligations, including a restraint of trade clause.

There will usually be a provision in the contract of employment for either party to give notice. If there is not a notice clause, then the employee is entitled to the amount of notice specified by statute. Wages in lieu of notice can be accepted.

Termination without notice by the employer (summary dismissal) is a breach of contract unless there are grounds which the law regards as sufficient to justify the termination - for example gross misconduct and extreme carelessness on the part of an employee.

If the summary dismissal was not justified then this amounts to wrongful dismissal. The employee is entitled to terminate the contract without notice if the employer breaks an important term of the contract. Where this happens, the employer is said to have 'repudiated' the contract by his breach enabling the employee to treat the contract as ended without notice.

There are differing opinions among lawyers as to whether or not the repudiation by one party has to be accepted by the other before the contract is terminated.

If an employee has one year's continuous employment with the employer at the effective date of termination, the employee is entitled to a written statement giving the reasons for the dismissal. This must be provided by the employer within 14 days of a request being received. If an employer does not comply with this request, the employee may complain to an Employment Tribunal.

The remedy for wrongful dismissal is to claim damages. The ordinary rules of contract law are applied to decide the amount of damages. Therefore, the employee can claim damages to compensate for losses which arise in the ordinary course of events from the breach itself and also for losses which it was reasonable for both parties to foresee as being likely to arise from the breach. If there has been no loss, the employee cannot claim compensation.

An employee cannot generally claim damages for the manner of dismissal. The House of Lord case of Johnson v. Unisys Ltd (2001) reaffirmed this long established principle. This particular case involved a long serving employee who was summarily dismissed outside the employer's disciplinary procedure, then admitted to a mental hospital and was subsequently unable to find work in the software industry.

The House of Lords said that damages for wrongful dismissal cannot include compensation for the manner of the dismissal, for the employee's injured feelings or for the loss the employee may sustain from the fact the dismissal itself may make it more difficult to get fresh employment.

The damages awarded may be reduced if the employee fails to take steps to mitigate their loss, i.e. by actively seeking alternative employment. The damages are also reduced by the amount of tax he would have paid and other benefits received, such as sick pay, income support and unemployment benefit.

9

UNFAIR DISMISSAL

The majority of cases taken to an employment tribunal are in respect of alleged unfair dismissal. To claim unfair dismissal, the employer must have terminated the contract of employment, either orally, in writing or by his conduct.

In many cases it is clear that a dismissal has taken place. However, dismissal includes circumstances where the employee has resigned and claims constructive dismissal. Constructive dismissal requires the employer to commit a fundamental breach of an employee's contract. This chapter provides a step by step guide to the law concerning unfair dismissal.

Not all workers are afforded protection from being unfairly dismissed. A self-employed person does not have the same rights as an employee and cannot claim for unfair dismissal (see Chapter 1).

Having established that the worker is an employee, there are several conditions that must apply to enable a claim for unfair dismissal to be pursued.

Do you have a claim?
- *Have you been employed long enough?*
- *Have you been dismissed?*
- *Were you under 65 or below the normal retirement age for your job when dismissed?*
- *Are you in an excluded category?*
- *Are you within the time limit for making a claim?*

If you were dismissed after 1 June 1999, you must in most cases have served one year's continuous employment with your employer to bring a claim for unfair dismissal. Holiday, maternity leave or sick leave does not break the continuity of employment.

The date on which continuous employment starts is written in your contract of employment. If not, it usually starts from your first day at work, although in some circumstances other periods of employment count towards continuous employment.

There are some situations where there is no length of service requirement, e.g. where you have been dismissed for any of the reasons deemed automatically unfair.

It is generally clear when there has been a dismissal as there will have been express words used by the employer to terminate the contract of employment. Rarer are occasions when the employee may choose to leave and it is accepted as a dismissal. This is called 'constructive dismissal'.

As well as being below the age of retirement, you must normally work in the UK, although a recent case established that an employment tribunal may be able to hear a claim provided the company is based in the United Kingdom even if the employee works abroad. The unfair dismissal provisions do not apply to certain excluded groups: policemen, share fishermen or domestic servants.

You must make a claim for unfair dismissal within three months of the date of your dismissal. Applications received after the time limit are rarely accepted. You must submit the application to the employment tribunal within the time limit, even if you are still going through your company's complaints procedure.

The three month limit starts, if you are given notice (whether you are required to work your notice or not) from the day your notice period ends. If you are paid in lieu of notice, the period starts from the actual date of the dismissal. If you are dismissed without notice the period runs from the date of the dismissal.

Was your dismissal fair?

It is for the employer to show that the reason for dismissal was at least potentially fair. The relevant legislation contains categories of reasons which are either automatically unfair or potentially fair.

Dismissals relating to the following are regarded as automatically unfair:

▸ trade union membership or activities
▸ pregnancy or any reason connected with pregnancy
▸ for a spent conviction

- in connection with transfer of an undertaking
- health and safety cases
- refusal to work on Sunday
- the making of a protected disclosure (see Chapter 5)
- on the grounds of an assertion of a statutory right

Provided the employee can show a tribunal that they were dismissed for one of the reasons which are regarded as automatically unfair, then the claim for unfair dismissal should succeed.

The legislation stipulates that the following reasons are potentially fair reasons for dismissal:

- capabilities or qualifications
- the employee's conduct
- redundancy
- statutory requirements, i.e. a driving licence for a driver
- some other substantial reason (see below)

In addition to a dismissal being for a fair reason, the employer must have acted reasonably in treating it as a reason for dismissing the employee. The employer will be able to show that he acted reasonably if, in all the circumstances of the case, the decision to dismiss was within 'the band of reasonable responses which a reasonable employer would adopt'. This is often known as the reasonable responses test.

The fact that an employer has a range of responses that are potentially fair, as opposed to just one, makes it difficult to tell definitively whether an employee has been unfairly dismissed.

Procedural fairness is one of the key factors in deciding whether or not the employer has acted reasonably. The current code of the Advisory, Conciliation & Arbitration Service (ACAS) on disciplinary and grievance procedure is a bit like the highway code for road users. A failure to observe any provision of the code does not by itself render the employer liable to proceedings.

However, in any proceedings before an employment tribunal any provision of the code which appears to be relevant to any question arising is admissible in evidence and is required to be taken into account in deciding that issue.

It is argued that the Employment Act 2002, alters the way dismissals are judged. Where an employer fails to follow the statutory dismissal and disciplinary procedures contained in the Act, a dismissal will be automatically unfair.

The Act also specifies that an employer's failure to follow a procedure other than the statutory procedure will not by itself make a dismissal unfair, provided the employer can show that following the appropriate procedure would have made no difference to the decision to dismiss.

The sections of the Act dealing with the minimum disciplinary standards will go out to consultation during summer 2003, with implementation expected in April 2004. The Advisory, Conciliation & Arbitration Service (ACAS) will be invited to revise its code on disciplinary and grievance procedures.

Guidance will be provided by collaboration between ACAS, Small Business Service and other advisory groups.

Provided the minimum standards as set out in the Act are met and the dismissal is otherwise fair, procedural shortcomings can be disregarded. Before the Act, where an unfair procedure was used to bring about a dismissal, that dismissal would have been unfair even if compliance with a fair procedure would still have led to the dismissal. The reasoning behind this change is in keeping with the overall theme of trying to reduce the number of claims going to a tribunal by removing arguments over minor breaches of procedure.

However, it should be remembered that a tribunal could decide that although the employer complied with minimum statutory requirements, in the circumstances of the particular case, because another procedure was not followed, then the employer had not acted reasonably.

Let us examine in more detail the potentially fair reasons for dismissal:

Capability

Your capability is assessed by reference to skill, aptitude, health or any other physical or mental quality. It can be based on the inability to reach the required standard or not being able to do the job which you were able to do because of illness or accident.

An employment tribunal will expect an employer to treat these two situations differently. It may be reasonable to warn an employee that he should improve his standards but it may not be reasonable behaviour to warn a genuinely sick employee that he must get well or else. In situations of sickness, the starting point is the reason for the illness. If sickness is as a result of working conditions then the employer must take steps to alleviate the condition or provide alternative employment. A risk of illness may be a fair reason for dismissal if the employee has an important role and a sudden illness could be dangerous to those around him.

The law distinguishes between persistent short term illness and a single long term illness. In the case of regular short term illness, it would be appropriate to issue warnings of the consequences of continual absence. As regards long term illness, the nature and length of the illness may frustrate the contract and so there is no need to consider unfair dismissal as the contract will have come to an end by operation of law.

A tribunal will often consider that training or increased management will be the appropriate first responses to an employee that is not performing to the required standard. It will be rare that dismissal is a reasonable first response for poor performers.

Qualifications

Failing to reach a standard an employee does not know about is not a fair reason to dismiss him. A standard does not however have to remain static, but a reasonable employer should train and allow for the employee to meet the new standard.

When considering incapability, it must relate to the job an employee is employed to do as laid down by his contract. The employer must produce evidence that he genuinely believed, on reasonable grounds, that the employee was incapable. This might be a comparison with other employees doing the same work or a consideration of sales figures or other performance indications.

It would be unfair not to inform the employee that the level of his work was falling or failing to reach acceptable standards. The employer should therefore give an employee a warning so that he has an opportunity to reach the required level. Sometimes, a single act which falls below required standards can be sufficient if the consequences are serious.

Conduct

Misconduct is a common reason for dismissal. It is up to the employer to provide evidence. An employer must go through a proper process, for example investigating prior to dismissing an employee for misconduct. Any investigation by the employer will be examined by a tribunal and consideration will be given as to how far it complies with the minimum statutory requirements and any applicable code produced by ACAS.

Statutes do not lay down the seriousness of misconduct which can justify dismissal but principles have emerged from cases. The misconduct does not have to be gross, only substantial to the circumstances, which means that in certain cases a relatively minor act can justify dismissal.

However, employers must be very careful before dismissing an employee for an act that does not constitute gross misconduct as the tribunal will expect an employer to take reasonable steps first to ensure that the misconduct is not repeated.

Neither does the conduct does have to be blameworthy, for example where a worker refused to retrain when all machines of a particular type went out of service. Although the employee may not be to blame, dismissal in such circumstances can be justified.

Courts have decided that where a driver refuses to retrain on a different Class of HGV when a particular class has gone out of service, it was regarded as fair although the driver was not to blame for the dismissal.

It would be impossible to go through every act of misconduct but the following are some of the main examples of misconduct which justify dismissal:

- Absenteesim and lateness
- Disloyality
- Disobedience
- Violence and fighting

Conduct outside employment:

An employment tribunal will usually only consider conduct within employment. However, there are circumstances where conduct committed outside employment can justify dismissal. It may be justified where the circumstances reflect on the relationship between the employer and employee so that all trust and confidence in the worker is lost.

The employer must show that the conduct outside working hours has a direct effect on the employment relationship. It would be fair to dismiss if the conduct makes him:

- unsuitable for the job; or
- unacceptable to other employees; or
- likely to cause potential harm to the business.

In some cases, the dismissal of someone for their conduct outside of work is fairly self-explanatory. It would be fair to dismiss a lorry driver who has been convicted of drink-driving if there is no alternative work he can do.

Disciplinary and Grievance Procedures: The ACAS Code and the effect of The Employment Act 2002

The latest ACAS code came into effect on 4 September 2000. It states that when drawing up disciplinary rules, the aim should be to specify clearly and concisely those that are necessary for the efficient and safe performance of work and for the maintenance of satisfactory relations within the workforce and between workers and management.

It is unlikely that any one set of disciplinary rules can cover all the circumstances that may arise. However, it is usual that rules would cover issues such as misconduct, sub-standard performance, harassment or victimisation, misuse of company facilities including computer facilities (eg, e-mail and the internet), poor timekeeping and unauthorised absences.

The rules will not be exactly the same for every company as they will depend on the particular circumstances, such as the type of work, working conditions and size of the workplace. Whatever set of rules are eventually drawn up they should not be so general as to be meaningless.

Rules should be set out clearly and concisely in writing and be readily available to all workers, for example in handbooks or on company intranet sites.

When drawing up and applying a procedure regarding disciplinary procedures, the ACAS code states that employers should have regard to the requirements of natural justice. Before any disciplinary hearing, an employee should be informed of any allegations being made against him/her together with supporting evidence. The employee should be given the opportunity to challenge the allegations and evidence before decisions are reached.

Workers should also be given the right of appeal against any decisions taken. Depending on the outcome of the procedure some form of disciplinary action may be taken.

The ACAS code suggests:

▼ *A first verbal warning*
   where the infringement by the employee is not major.

▼ *A first written warning*
   where the employee has failed to improve while a previous warning is in operation.

▼ *Final written warning*

It would usually be expected that these warnings expire after a period of time, so that they do not continue to affect an employee's personnel record.

The Employment Act 2002

The Employment Act 2002, which is expected to be implemented in full by April 2004 aims to build constructive employment relations and reduce the need for litigation by introducing minimum internal disciplinary and grievance procedures. The procedures will be implied into each employee's contract of employment and must be included in the written statement of terms.

Employees and employers will be expected to comply with any Statutory Codes in respect of disciplinary procedures.

The following is a summary of the minimum dismissal and disciplinary procedures as contained in the Act:

Dismissal and Disciplinary Procedures

Step 1: Statement of grounds for action and invitation to meeting:

▼ *the employer must set out in writing the employee's alleged misconduct*

▼ *the employer must send the statement to the employee and invite the employee to attend a meeting to discuss the matter*

Step 2: Meeting

▼ *the meeting must take place before action is taken except in the case of suspension*

▼ *the meeting must not take place unless the employee has been informed of the basis for the contents of the statement of alleged conduct and the employee has been given a reasonable opportunity to consider his response to that information.*

▼ *the employee must take all reasonable steps to attend*

▼ *after the meeting, the employer must inform the employee of his decision and notify him of the right to appeal against the decision if he is not satisfied with it*

Step 3: Appeal

▼ *if the employee wishes to appeal he must inform the employer*

▼ *if the employee informs the employer of his wish to appeal, the employer must invite him to attend a further meeting*

▼ *the employee must take all reasonable steps to attend*

▼ *the meeting need not take place before dismissal or disciplinary action takes effect*

▼ *where practical, the appeal meeting should be held by an individual more senior to the person who conducted the first meeting and who was unconnected with the first meeting*

The standard grievance procedure follows the same three step process:

1. The employee sets out in writing to the employer the nature of the grievance
2. The employer must invite the employee to attend a meeting to discuss the grievance
3. If the employee wishes to appeal, he must inform the employer

There are some general requirements with respect to the above procedures. Each step of the action must be taken without unreasonable delay. The timing and location of the meetings must be reasonable, and must provide both sides with the opportunity to explain their cases.

In order to understand the main principles of disciplinary procedure, consider the following example of Richard Change and his dismissal by Bumble & Co Solicitors.

Richard Change joined Bumble & Co Solicitors two years ago to manage their Property Litigation department. The decision had been taken to streamline the department by bringing together its two teams within the firm's main office in Bumbletown.

Richard Change was invited to a meeting with the Personnel Manager, Mr Cutter, to discuss the logistics of merging the two property teams.

On arrival at the meeting with Mr Cutter, Richard is greeted by the departmental head Wilfred Summers, a person he did not expect to be at the meeting. Mr Cutter explains that the meeting will consider allegations that have been made against Richard by some members of his team.

After a brief discussion, Mr Cutter announces that Richard would receive a written warning because of his misconduct. A month later, Richard is dismissed by Bumble & Co.

The actions of the Personnel Manager at Bumble & Co fall short of the minimum standards as set out in the Employment Act 2002. It appears that Richard was given no written notice of the allegations and so had no opportunity to consider his response to the information. He was invited to attend a meeting but he believed it was called to discuss departmental matters.

Redundancy

Redundancy means the requirement for work of a particular kind has ceased in a place where the employee was employed. Employers are required not to dismiss workers unfairly when they make redundancies. In order to act lawfully, employers must either follow agreed procedures in selecting employees for redundancy or adopt a procedure which would be regarded as objectively fair.

Statutory Restriction

Statutory Restriction occurrs where an employee can no longer continue to work in the position which he held without contravention by himself or the employer of a duty or restriction imposed by law, e.g.in a situation where a lorry driver loses his driving licence.

Some other substantial reason

This is in effect a catch all reason in that if the reason does not fall within the first four categories it will be caught by this one. The two most common situations which arise in tribunals are business needs and pressure from third parties.

Remedies for Unfair Dismissal and Calculating Compensation

There are a number of remedies available to an applicant successful in his claim for unfair dismissal:

▼ Reinstatement
▼ Re-engagement
▼ Financial Compensation

Reinstatement is an order that the employer shall treat the employee in all respects as if he has not been dismissed and must include all the benefits payable in the period since his dismissal. In using its discretion to make a reinstatement order, a tribunal must have regard to:

a) the wishes of the complainant
b) whether it is practicable for the employer to comply with the order
c) whether it would be just to make the order if there has been contributory conduct

If the tribunal declines to make an order for reinstatement, it must then consider re-engagement. Such an order means that the employee is returned to a comparable job rather than his old job, but the job must be as favourable as the old one .

The tribunal will take into account similar factors to those considered regarding reinstatement. There are relatively few cases where orders for reinstatement or for re-engagement are made. The main remedy for unfair dismissal is financial compensation.

Basic Award:

The basic award is to compensate the employee for the loss of his job.

It is based on the employee's age and years of service.

> ▾ *Service below the age of 22: half a week's pay per year of service*
>
> ▾ *Service between 22 and 41: one week's pay per year of service*
>
> ▾ *Service over the age of 41: one and a half week's pay per year of service*

The above is subject to a statutory maximum which is at present is £260 per week. For example, suppose you gave 10 years service from the age of 25 to 35. The basic award would be 10 x £260 = £2,600

The award can be reduced for:

▸ Conduct - even if the conduct did not contribute to the dismissal

▸ The unreasonable refusal of an offer of reinstatement

▸ Any redundancy pay received

▸ Any ex gratia payments

The award cannot be reduced because of behaviour conducted after dismissal.

Compensatory award:

A compensatory award compensates the employee for the loss he has suffered as a result of the dismissal. The present statutory maximum is £53,500. When considering a compensatory award, the tribunal will look at a number of factors including immediate loss of earnings; future loss of earnings; loss of fringe benefits; expenses in looking for work; loss of pension rights; and the manner of the dismissal.

Additional Award

Where the employer has ignored an order for reinstatement or for re-engagement, or the dismissal was discriminatory, the tribunal may make an additional award. This is in addition to any basic and compensatory award.

The award will be between 26 week's pay and 52 week's pay, up to a current maximum of £13,520 after applying the statutory limit of £260 per week.

10

RESTRAINT OF TRADE CLAUSES IN EMPLOYMENT CONTRACTS

When an employee leaves an employer there will undoubtedly be information of a confidential nature, which if given to a competitor could undermine the business. An employee owes a duty of faithful service to his employer and part of that duty is not to divulge or otherwise misuse, confidential information. This duty is either implied or expressly stated in the contract of employment.

However, to properly protect a business most companies use express clauses. These clauses are known as restraint of trade clauses or restrictive covenants, and are contained within the contract of employment.

The purpose of restrictive covenants is to limit potentially unfair competition by employees taking advantage of business information and client contacts gained from their previous employment.

The most common clauses are:

▸ Non-solicitation covenants which aim to prevent the former employee from soliciting the clients of the employer.

▸ Non-dealing covenants, which aim to prevent the former employee from dealing with the clients of the employer, regardless of whether or not the former employee makes the initial approach.

▸ Area covenants which attempt to prevent the former employee from working in the same type of business in which he worked for the employer within a defined area for a specified period of time.

▸ Preventing the former employee from working for a business rival.

▸ Non-solicitation of other employees, which prevents any former employee from enticing work colleagues away from the former employer.

For a restraint of trade clause to be enforceable an employer must show that the clause is reasonable. What is regarded as reasonable will depend upon the specific circumstances of each case.

The attitude of the courts to restraint clauses has often depended on whether it is a 'non-employment' clause, which attempts to prevent the employee from working in a particular type of work or location, or a 'non-dealing' clause which seeks to prevent the use of contacts gained while working for the employer.

Courts are reluctant on grounds of public policy to place restrictions on workers' capacity to earn their living as they choose.

It could be argued that is there is no need for such clauses in a modern free market economy. If an employee is not good at his job then one can assume that customers are unlikely to follow him. On the other hand if an employee is good at his job and popular with clients then customers are likely to follow him and it would thus be in the interests of the employer to try and retain that individual.

For a clause to be enforceable the employer needs to show that he has some recognisable interest to protect, such as a secret process, a trade secret, or customer connections, and any disclosure could damage his business.

The clause should not restrict the former employee's activities more than is absolutely necessary. For this reason, if a clause is drafted too widely so as to unreasonably restrict an employee's activities, then the court will decide that the clause is not enforceable and cannot be relied upon by the employer.

The following example illustrates this point.

McBeal Solicitors employed Richard Fish as a law clerk at their office in Bristol. Within his contract there is a covenant which says that on the termination of his employment he must not for a period of 2 years, work in or be concerned with the legal profession anywhere within the postal district of Bristol and Bath or solicit any person who had been a client of the firm while he worked there.

The covenant is drafted too broadly and gives more protection than necessary. This clause would prevent Richard Fish from working in any part of the legal profession, such as working for local government or within a company legal department. A court would regard such a clause as unreasonable.

A restrictive covenant may be regarded as unreasonable because of other factors. The length of time the restraint is in place as well as the geographical restriction are relevant considerations.

In the case of Richard Fish, the period of the restriction - two years - is likely to be considered unreasonable. A period of between six to twelve months is often acceptable, depending on the facts.

Although restraint clauses can be enforced in respect of an employer's customers, a court is only likely to allow such protection where the employee has established a relationship with the customers concerned as this is the only real situation where there is a danger that the customers will follow the employee when he leaves.

Richard Fish was employed as a law clerk and so it may well be that he was not at a level where he would have established a relationship with the clients such as would make them follow him on his departure. This highlights the important factor of employee seniority when considering whether such a clause is enforceable.

It may appear that it is difficult to draft a valid restraint of trade provision in an employment contract. This is true to some extent as courts do not like placing a restriction on an employee's future job prospects. However, there are ways the courts can save such a clause.

It might consider the reality and effect of the provision. In the case of Hollis & Co v. Stocks (2000), a small firm of solicitors attempted to restrict an assistant solicitor for twelve months from working within ten miles of the firm's office. The clause did not define what the individual was prevented from doing.

The Court of Appeal interpreted the clause in question as one which restricted the individual from working as a solicitor, since this was the clear intention of the parties. The courts do not often interpret ambiguous clauses in this way and will only do so when they can determine what must have been the common intention of the parties.

Another way of saving a restraint clause is to strike out the offending parts and leave the elements which are reasonable and enforceable. This is known as the 'blue pencil technique'.

The test works on the basis that if the offending elements of the clause can be deleted and, if it still makes sense, then the remaining part will be valid. To illustrate how the courts might use the blue pencil technique, consider the following example:

Sharon and the Blue Rinse Salon

Sharon works as a hairdresser at the Blue Rinse Salon in Central London. Larry, her employer, required her to sign a contract of employment when she started at the salon that included a restraint of trade clause. In the contract, Sharon is prevented for a period of two years from working as a hairdresser on her own account or for any other salon within a 6 mile radius of the Blue Rinse Salon.
Neither must she solicit clients of the salon for a period of four months after leaving the Blue Rinse Salon. Sharon has been offered a new job as a stylist at the Top Cat Salon, which is 3 miles away.

The geographical restriction would most likely be regarded as excessive. It goes beyond what is necessary to protect the legitimate business interests of the Blue Rinse Salon. This is partly because of its London location. The fact that there are many salons in London means that Sharon's departure to another firm would not be as damaging as it would be in a situation where she was working in a small village and left to join the only other salon in the area.

In the case of a small village, the two salons would probably be competing for the same customers. To allow the clause above would effectively force Sharon out of central London. However, the restriction on soliciting Larry's clients for a period of four months may be considered reasonable.

If these restrictions are contained in the same clause then the restriction on soliciting clients would also be unenforceable. However, if the restrictions were drafted in separate clauses, then a court might use the blue pencil technique to remove the geographical restriction and still leave an enforceable non-solicitation clause.

There are other ways in which a restrictive covenant cannot be enforced, such as instances where the employer commits a repudiatory breach of contract. To help understand this point, consider the example which follows:

Fred Revenue and No Messing Collections

Fred Revenue was employed by the debt collection company
No Messing Ltd. Fred had been employed for six months as
their Credit Manager. Fred's contract contains restrictive
covenants as to the contacts whom he may approach after the
termination of his contract.
Suddenly, with no prior notice, he was called in to see his
supervisor and confronted with an allegation that he had
"upset" a colleague in the credit department. Fred was given
no detail of what he was supposed to have done and to whom,
and he was told to leave immediately without being given the
required one month's notice. Fred cannot recall having an
inappropriate conversation.

If the employer has committed a breach of contract which goes to the root of the contract, for example a breach of the implied duty of trust and confidence, then the employee can regard the contract as ended.

In the event that an employer breaches the contract then the court will not consider it fair for the employee to continue to be bound by the restrictive covenants. Therefore, in some circumstances, the court will hold that the restrictive covenants do not apply.

In Fred's case, No Messing has committed a repudiatory breach of the contract and so it is arguable that it would not be able to enforce any restraint of trade clauses. Even if Fred had been given notice he could still argue a repudiatory breach of contract with the effect that any restraint clauses do not apply. It could be argued that No Messing has acted so badly it has undermined the implied term as to mutual trust and confidence.

The breach of contract must be significant. In the case of Cantor Fitzgerald International v. Callaghan (1999), a company failed to pay employees £8,000 to meet tax liabilities arising from a company loan. The Court of Appeal said that it was not only the amount involved which should be considered but the motivation of the employer. So a deliberate refusal to pay would be different to an error on the part of the employer.

Having considered the difficulties in drafting an enforceable restraint of trade clause, let us consider an example which the courts may regard as reasonable.

Restraint Clause

1.(1).During the course of your employment, it is likely that you will form close working relationships with the Company's clients, professional intermediaries who introduce clients and with members of staff. The relationship between the Company and its clients, professional intermediaries and staff is a valuable asset and is reasonable for the Company to seek to protect. You therefore agree that to protect the Company's legitimate business interests both during your employment and after its termination, you will not directly or indirectly:

i. for a period of six months from termination of your employment, solicit, entice or otherwise encourage any key employee to terminate his relationship with the Company who at the time or within a six months preceding the termination of your employment was employed by the Company;

ii. for a period of six months from termination of your employment, employ, engage in office or be in partnership in similar business relationship with any key employee who at the time of or within six months preceding termination of your employment was employed by the Company;

iii. for a period of six months from termination of your employment, conduct yourself in any way calculated to attract business to yourself or to any other organisation from any person or organisation you had contact with during the course of your employment in the twelve months preceding the termination of your employment.

1.(2). Each paragraph of 1(1) is a separate and distinct undertaking and may be severed accordingly.

1.(3). The term 'key employee' referred to in 1(1).i. is defined as....................

Although the courts will consider the nature and scope of the employer's business, as well as the employee's status and responsibilities, it can be said that the above restraint clause is drafted in such a way that should make it enforceable.

It sets out to protect the legitimate interests of the company, which are the relationships between clients and staff. The clauses are not vague and do not appear to be excessive in terms of the period of the restraint. Furthermore, the clauses have been drafted separately.

For example, if the courts felt that clause 1(1) iii. was not reasonable it could use the blue pencil test and strike out this part, leaving 1(1) i and 1(1) ii as enforceable covenants. Care must taken be to ensure that 1(3) defines what is meant by a 'key employee', i.e. it might refer to a senior manager or director.

A clause could be included which states that where a clause is deemed unenforceable due to unreasonableness, then the court can decide what is reasonable. So, for example, if a clause preventing the soliciting of clients for a period of two years was regarded as unreasonable, then the court can decide what period of time would be reasonable.

Enforcing a restraint clause

If an employee breaches a restraint of trade clause, the usual remedy is to seek an injunction to prevent breach of the restraint of trade clause. These can be expensive, particularly if the court subsequently ruled in favour of the ex-employee due to the unreasonableness of the clause(s).

Before taking action against an ex-employee, the employer may wish to write to him and request an undertaking that he will not continue to breach the covenant. This may be appropriate where the breach has been minor and has not caused much damage.

If the employer chooses to seek an injunction, then an application to a court will be necessary. The employer may want to apply for an interim injunction before the matter is considered at the full hearing. This would prevent any immediate breaches of the covenant and would protect the employer's interests because his business might be seriously damaged by the time of the full court hearing.

Given that the majority of restraint covenants are not for long periods of time, injunctive relief may be difficult to obtain.

If the employer does not seek an injunction, he could claim damages to compensate the loss he has incurred as a result of the breach. However in practice it may be difficult for the employer to quantify the loss in financial terms.

11.

DISCRIMINATION

United Kingdom law recognises three types of discrimination:-
▸ Sex discrimination
▸ Race discrimination
▸ Disability discrimination

Three main pieces of legislation cover existing discrimination law:-
▸ The Sex Discrimination Act 1975
▸ The Race Relations Act 1976
▸ The Disability Act 1995
There is also a European Directive on Equal Treatment.

The provisions of the 1975 and 1976 Acts are very similar and so much of the case law is interchangeable. The legislation outlaws direct and indirect discrimination, as well as victimisation.

The legislation on discrimination covers all aspects of the employment relationship from the recruitment stage, right through the working relationship until to termination of the job. The rights given to workers by this legislation extend to 'an individual working under a contract for service' (ie an independent self-employed contractor) as well as to an employee. No minimum period of employment is required to permit a claim for discrimination.

At present, it is not unlawful to discriminate against a person on the basis of their age, but legislation will be introduced in this area by December 2006.

Sex Discrimination
There are two types of descrimination - direct and indirect discrimination.

Direct discrimination
The majority of claims for sex discrimination are brought by women,

although men can also claim sex discrimination. Direct discrimination occurs when a person is treated less favourably on the grounds of sex.

A person not only has to show that the treatment is different, but also that the treatment is unfavourable. An example of direct discrimination might be in a case where a female employee is told that she would have been promoted but for her being a woman. The test applied is therefore would the employee have been treated more favourably but for his/her sex?

Indirect Sex Discrimination

Indirect discrimination occurs where an employer applies a requirement or condition to a woman, which they also apply to a man, but:

- The proportion of women who are able to comply with it is considerably smaller than the proportion of men; and
- The employer cannot justify it; and
- The condition is to the complainant's detriment because she is unable to comply with it.

Such indirect discrimination may equally occur conversely where a man is the victim of the case.

The key element is whether the requirement is justified in view of the duties to be performed. Where such a condition or requirement is applied and a claim of discrimination is made against an employer, the employer must show that the condition or requirement is justified on economic, administrative or other grounds.

A balance has to be made between the discriminatory effect of the condition and the reasonable needs of the employer. The courts will ask themselves how many will suffer as a result and how seriously will they do so.

A successful claim for sex discrimination will depend on the victim being able to show that he/she has been treated less favourably than a person of the opposite sex. The need for comparison has created difficulties in deciding what is the 'comparative group'.

There are legal cases which have attempted to assist in defining the comparative group.

In one such case, the courts considered the question of indirect discrimination where a college applied a requirement for those wanting to apply for a post of senior lecturer. The applicants had to work full time at the college which was run by the local authority.

It was claimed that the requirement was discriminatory and statistics were produced to show that out of the academic staff, 21.8% of women could apply compared with 46.7% of men. It was decided that the comparative group was too wide. The group should have been those staff with the necessary qualifications to apply rather than all academic staff at the college.

Deciding the appropriate comparative group is a complex issue. However, what it aims to achieve is to compare like with like.

Clothing and Appearance:

Tribunals tend to consider the rules on clothing and appearance as a whole. It takes a pragmatic approach, recognising that men and women are different therefore, it is expected that the rules will differ. Provided the employer enforces the rules even-handedly, they are unlikely to be regarded as discriminatory.

Job advertisements:

When advertising a position in a newspaper or magazine, an employer must consider the issue of discrimination. The responsibility not to discriminate also rests on the publisher. If there is discrimination, the Equal Opportunities Commission may take action to enforce the law. There are a number of things that an employer should consider when placing a job advertisement, including:

▾ *does the job description deter women from applying?*
▾ *are there any conditions or requirements within the advertisement which could be discriminatory?*

Interviews:

Discrimination can often take place at an interview where men and women are asked different questions.

Fiona and Ancient & Co

Fiona goes for an interview for the post of trainee accountant at Ancient and Co. Mr Ancient asks Fiona questions about her plans to get married, have a family and whether or not she would be able to balance family life with work commitments. Fiona does not get the job and seeks advice about a claim for sex discrimination.

In the case of Fiona, she was asked unnecessary questions about her domestic circumstances which were not relevant to the job.

The Sex Discrimination Act 1975 does not allow positive discrimination, i.e. appointing a person because of their sex, but what is permissible is 'positive action'. Examples of positive action include encouraging women to apply for positions in which they are under represented.

Article 2(4) of the Equal Treatment Directive allows for the introduction of 'measures to promote equal opportunity for men and women, in particular by removing existing inequalities which affect women's opportunities'. Amendments to Article 141 also allows for EU member states to adopt measures which provide for 'specific advantage' to an under-represented sex in order to achieve full equality in practice. Such measures in reality amount to positive discrimination.

With the introduction of the Sex Discrimination (Indirect Discrimination and Burden of Proof) Regulations 2001 (SI 20001/2660), a person making a complaint of sex discrimination merely has to establish the facts of the complaint.

As the recent case of Barton v. Investec Henderson Crosthwaithe Securities Ltd (April 2003) confirmed, the applicant has to prove facts from which inferences could be drawn that the respondent had treated the applicant less favourably on the basis of sex. The burden of proof then moves to the person accused of discrimination. They have to prove on the balance of probabilities that the treatment was not in any way based on the ground of sex.

Sexual harassment

Sexual harassment is unlawful direct discrimination. It occurs when conduct towards men/women is unwanted, unreasonable and offensive. The conduct must be such that the victim feels intimidated or the subject of hostility or is humiliated. Provided the employee has made it clear that the conduct is unwelcome, any repetition could amount to harassment.

There are difficulties in saying whether or not certain types of behaviour amount to harassment as some people will find some behaviour offensive while others may not.

Race Discrimination

The provisions of the Race Relations Act 1976 are very similar to the Sex Discrimination Act 1975. Race discrimination occurs where an employer or potential employer treats a person less favourably than he treats or would treat others on racial grounds. The 1976 Act defines 'racial grounds' as 'colour, race, nationality or ethnic or national origins'.

There have been many cases which have attempted to define 'ethnic origin'. In the case of Mandla v. Dowell Lee (1983) the House of Lords laid down a number of conditions to be considered for any group which wishes to fall within the Act. The conditions to be considered are:

- *A long shared history*
- *A cultural tradition of its own*
- *A common geographical origin*
- *A common language*
- *A common literature*
- *Being a minority, or an oppressed or dominant group within a community*

The Court applied these factors in Mandla v. Dowell Lee and it was decided that Sikhs are an ethnic group. Courts since have decided that:

- *Jews are an ethnic group*
- *Gypsies are an ethnic group*
- *Rastafarians are **not** an ethnic group*
- *Jehovah's Witnesses are **not** an ethnic or racial group*
- *The Race Relations Act covers Welsh people*
- *Scottish and English people are covered by the reference to 'national origins' instead of 'ethnic origins'*

Indirect Race Discrimination

Indirect discrimination occurs if on racial grounds the employer applies to one person a requirement or condition which they apply or would apply equally to persons not of the same racial group but:

- it is such that the proportion of persons in that racial

group who can comply with it is considerably smaller than the proportion of people not of that racial group who can comply with it; and

- the employer cannot justify it; and
- it is to the detriment of that other person because he cannot comply.

The Race Relations Act 1976 (Amendment Regulations 2003), inserted an addition to the definition of indirect race discrimination. These regulations also insert new clauses in respect of the burden of proof in race relations cases, similar to those introduced by the Sex Discrimination (Indirect Discrimination and Burden of Proof) Regulations 2001 mentioned earlier.

Mr Hammad and Fine Wines Ltd
Mr Hammad is a Muslim and is forbidden by his religion from consuming alcohol. He applies for a job at a local wine company but is not successful. He claims race discrimination.
Fine Wines successfully defend the claim as the position for which Mr Hammad applied included wine tasting and this was a necessary requirement of the job because the employee had to be able to talk about wine and have a first hand knowledge of different wines.

The case of Mr Hammad is an example of the employer being able to justify a requirement.

Victimisation
Victimisation occurrs where an employee is treated less favourably by his/her employer because he/she has either brought proceedings, has given evidence in, done anything or intends to do something relating to, the discrimination legislation.

Vicarious Liability
An employer will usually be held responsible for the acts (or omissions) committed by its employees in the course of their employment.

This principle of vicarious liability applies to sex and race discrimination under s41 of the Sex Discrimination Act 1975 and s32 of the Race Relations Act 1976.

Early cases of vicarious liability allowed employers to avoid liability by arguing that it was not part of the employee's job to commit the acts complained of and therefore such acts were not committed in the course of their employment.

More recent cases have developed a broader definition of the words 'in the course of employment'. An example of this wider definition occurred in a recent case where it was decided that since work related social functions are an extension of employment, a male police officer who sexually harassed a female colleague at both an after work gathering and an organised leaving party was acting 'in the course of his employment'.

The extent to which an employer can be held responsible for discrimination was increased in the unusual case of Burton and Rhule v. De Vere Hotels (1996). In this case, a function room was hired to a third party who booked comedian Bernard Manning as the guest speaker. Two Afro-Caribbean waitresses working at the function were subjected to racially and sexually offensive remarks.

They complained to the hotel management, their employer, who moved them away from working in that location. They then brought an action against their employer for racial harassment and succeeded. The reasoning behind this decision was that although the hotel apparently acted reasonably by moving the waitresses, the action was not enough. The hotel should have given thought to the risk of the event.

The harassment was foreseeable. The comedian is renowned for making racial remarks and the hotel had control over the situation. Therefore, in the circumstances the employer was held responsible. The House of Lords , which criticised the decision in June 2003,.did not specifically overrule it but did rule that an employer is not liable in respect of sex or race harassment of the employee by a third party unless the employer failed to prevent the harassment for a reason related to the sex or race of the employee.

Disability Discrimination

Under the Disability Discrimination Act 1995 an employer discriminates against a disabled person if: 'for reason which relates to the disabled person's disability, he treats him less favourably than he treats or would treat others and he cannot show that the treatment in question is justified.'

Disability is defined as being a physical or mental impairment which has a substantial and long-term adverse effect on the ability of a person to carry out normal day-to-day activities. The legislation only applies to companies employing 15 or more people. It imposes a duty on an employer to make reasonable adjustments, which includes widening doorways and other adjustments to premises, re-allocating some of the duties of the disabled person, transferring a disabled person to fill an existing vacancy, altering the employee's hours or place of work and modifying equipment.

In deciding what steps it is reasonable for an employer to take, regard is given to what is practicable, the financial or other costs and the resources available to the particular employer.

Fred River and Machines R Us Ltd

Machines R Us is a large company employing several hundred people. Fred is employed as a machine operator, operating a machine which requires him to be very dextrous. Fred has an accident while on a motorcycle and permanently loses the use of his left-hand making it difficult for him to operate his machine.

The company is very understanding and allows him extended sick leave while he is recovering from the accident. However, when Fred wants to return to his job on the machine the employer refuses. They say he would not be able to use the machinery. Fred argues that with a modification he would still be able to operate the tool and so perform his duties. There are no other positions within the company to which he could transfer and so Machines R Us asks Fred to leave.

In Fred's case, we would need to know the cost and practicability of making the modification. Also, having made the modification, would Fred still be able to operate the machine without there being a risk to the health and safety of Fred and his fellow employees?

An employer can justify, on the grounds of health and safety, a failure to comply with the duty to make reasonable adjustments.

Defences to Discrimination

It is a complete defence to sex and race discrimination to show that the discrimination occurred where sex or race is a genuine occupational qualification. Examples of genuine occupation include:

▶ physiology, dramatic performance; entertainment or authenticity

▶ for reasons of decency or privacy

▶ the work is in a private home and involves close physical or social contact

Remedies

A person can make a complaint to a tribunal and the usual remedy sought is compensation. There is no upper limit on the size of an award. Some recent high profile sex discrimination cases have illustrated the point that employers can leave themselves liable for a big payout if they breach the legislation.

A recent survey showed that in just one year a total of £3.53 million was awarded in discrimination cases. Approximately half of this sum was for sex discrimination, one third for race discrimination and a one fifth for disability discrimination.

Despite the headline catching awards, recent figures show that the median awards were:

▶ Sex discrimination £4,847

▶ Race discrimination £6,833

▶ Disability discrimination £5,175

An alternative remedy is for the tribunal to recommend that the employer takes action within a time period to remove the adverse effect of the discrimination. If within that specified period the employer does not comply with the recommendation, then the tribunal may make an order for, or increase the amount of, compensation.

12.

MAKING A CLAIM TO A TRIBUNAL

This chapter explains how employees can enforce their rights by making a complaint to an employment tribunal. To illustrate the procedure, we examine the case involving Fiona Buckingham, who makes a claim for sex discrimination. The forms that are used in a tribunal application are contained in the Appendices at the end of this book.

Before submitting a complaint to an employment tribunal, it is worth obtaining legal advice to check the merits of the claim. There are various places where free advice can be obtained, such as the local Citizens' Advice Bureau or Law Centre. Many law firms may also offer free legal surgeries.

With a time limit of three months in which to make your claim to a tribunal, it is vital to act quickly and assess whether you have the basis of a complaint. Employers should also seek advice at an early stage so that they are in a position to defend any proceedings brought by an employee.

The Employment Tribunal

An employment tribunal will hear claims of unfair dismissal, redundancy and discrimination. It can also hear claims relating to wages and terms and conditions of employment. An employment tribunal is like a court but less formal. The panel who hear the case do not wear wigs or gowns.

Usually, the tribunal consists of a legally qualified chairman, such as an experienced barrister, and two lay people who have experience in dealing with employment related problems.

Legal aid is not available for representation at an employment tribunal but it is possible to obtain legal expenses insurance to cover the costs of an unfair dismissal claim. Organisations such as the Commission for Racial Equality or the Equal Opportunities Commission may assist applicants with advice and representation. They might provide help where the case raises a question of principle or where a claim involves complicated issues and it would be unreasonable to expect an individual to handle his/her case unaided.

Proceedings in the employment tribunal are informal so it is not always necessary to be represented by a lawyer. About two thirds of applicants and a half of respondents are not represented by lawyers. Most people are capable of bringing or defending proceedings brought to an employment tribunal without legal representation.

Trade Unions, Citizens' Advice Bureaux and Law Centres are often available to provide free assistance with the presentation of a case.

Beginning proceedings

To begin proceedings, an employee needs to complete Form IT1. This form is reproduced in Appendix A. Form IT1 should then be sent to the Central Office of Employment Tribunals or to the appropriate Regional Office. The appropriate Regional Office will serve Form IT1 on the employer by ordinary post. If it is not received, then another copy will be sent by recorded delivery.

Form IT1 is used for all employment tribunal claims. Some of the questions are not relevant to particular claims.

Box 1: This should clearly identify all the complainants. If there is more than one complainant, they should all be listed.

Box 2: The date of birth of the complainant may be relevant to decide potential exclusion from the right to claim, the amount of a redundancy payment and the level of the basic award.

Box 4: This is important as it will indicate, for example, whether the employee has the qualifying period of continuous employment for unfair dismissal claims. Ensure that the effective date of termination is correct. In summary, the effective date of termination is:

i. where an employee is dismissed with notice, the date on which the notice expired;

ii. where the dismissal is lawfully carried out without notice, the date of that dismissal

iii. where the minimum notice period is longer than the notice which has in fact be given, the end of the period of proper minimum notice

iv. where a person is dismissed with payment in lieu of notice, the date the employee is told of the termination

v. in the case of a fixed term contract, the date when that fixed term expires without being renewed under the same contract

Box 5: The place of work may be important in deciding the right to a redundancy payment, or whether in refusing to move to another place of work an employee has disobeyed a reasonable instruction

Box 11: The details of the complaint are entered here. There is often not enough space so for clarity it may be better to type the details of the complaint on a separate sheet of paper and attach it to the form. Any relevant correspondence can also be attached. Form IT1 is the first document which the employment tribunal will see and so it is important to make a good impression. Try and avoid a statement of case which is incoherent and barely legible.

Box 10: This requests the applicant to state the remedy to be sought. The applicant is not bound by the answer. If an applicant indicates compensation, he/she may later decide to seek reinstatement or re-engagement.

Fiona Buckingham and Ran Dee Ltd

Fiona Buckingham works as Public Relations Executive at Ran Dee Ltd. which specialise in handling press releases and marketing for a number of corporate clients in the City.

Fiona is relatively junior and is supervised by Andy Handy, her line manager.

Between April and September 2003, Fiona was subjected to sexual harassment from Mr Handy. Fiona made it clear to Mr Handy that the sexual harassment was unwelcome. In October, Ran Dee Ltd conducted an investigation and concluded there was inconclusive evidence of harassment.

After Fiona's rejection of Mr Handy's advances she felt she was subjected to further discrimination.

In November, Fiona applied for promotion but was not selected.. The successful candidate was a man with fewer qualifications and experience. Fiona believes that but for the sexual harassment she suffered, she would have got the job.

Fiona decides to make a complaint to an employment tribunal. It is important that she carefully sets out the details of her complaint. Her complaint reads as follows:

IT1 - Fiona Buckingham - Details of Complaint:

1. I am employed by Ran Dee Ltd as a Public Relations Executive, having worked for them for four years. Mr Andy Handy is my line manager.

2. Between April and September 2003, when I was undertaking my work in the same office as Mr Handy, he sexually harassed me both physically and verbally. The harassment included the following:

- holding my arm and kissing my lips
- running his fingers up my legs to the tops of my thighs
- patting my bottom
- putting his hand under my skirt and feeling my buttocks
- asking if I was satisfied with my sex life
- standing so close to me that he touched the side of my breasts

3. I made it clear to Mr Handy that the above sexual harassment was unwelcome and I complained to Mr Handy's manager.

4. In October 2003, Ran Dee Ltd carried out an investigation into my allegations but the investigation concluded that the evidence of sexual harassment was inconclusive.

5. After I had rejected Mr Handy's sexual advances, he further discriminated against me by, among other things:

- excluding me from departmental meetings
- making derogatory comments about my appearance
- criticising my attitude towards the management
- telling me that I would not get promotion
- giving work to another more junior colleague without consulting me
- causing the working relationship to deteriorate

6. In November 2003, I applied for promotion for the position of Senior Public Relations Executive. The successful candidate was a man with fewer qualifications and less experience. I believe that but for the sexual harassment I suffered I would have been appointed.

7. The above treatment I experienced was a continuing course

of discrimination. If it is not accepted that there was a continuing course of discrimination, I will argue that it that it is just and equitable to allow the claim out of time.

8. Ran Dee Ltd refused to change my line manager or to take any action against Mr Handy.

9. In breach of the Equal Opportunities Commission Code of Practice and the EC Code of Practice, Ran Dee Ltd had no equal opportunities procedure to deal with sexual harassment.

10. As a result of the sexual harassment by Mr Handy, for which Ran Dee Ltd are liable, and their failure to take action to deal with it, I was subjected to a detriment on the grounds of my sex.

I claim:

▸ a declaration that I have suffered sex discrimination
▸ compensation for sex discrimination, including injury to my feelings.

Signed Fiona Buckingham   Dated 20 December 2003

There are no provisions within the Sex Discrimination Act which specifically deal with sexual harassment. However, the courts have decided that harassment is a form of direct discrimination.

According to her complaint, Fiona has suffered 'unwanted physical or verbal conduct directed against her on account of her sex'. In addition, she has suffered a detriment.

The details of Fiona's complaint state that the treatment that she received was a continuing course of discrimination. According to the Sex Discrimination Act, any act extending over a period shall be treated as done at the end of that period. This is important to remember in cases where there is a history of harassment over a long period. This could be relevant where the complaint might be out of time.

However, in discrimination cases, the period for filing a complaint may be extended if the tribunal thinks it is just and equitable to do so. In addition, the Sex Discrimination Act permits the period for presenting a complaint to be extended to six months where there has been persistent discrimination. In Fiona's case, she has presented her complaint within time.

Responding to the Claim

The Employer ('the Respondent') has 21 days from the date of receipt of Form IT1 to submit a Notice of Appearance on Form IT3. This form is shown at Appendix B. If the Respondent intends to contest the claim, Form IT3 is the form to use to enter a defence. If the Respondent does not return the Notice of Appearance within the allotted time, he cannot take part in the proceedings. The Respondent can ask for extra time to submit the Notice of Appearance.

In the case of Fiona and Ran Dee Ltd, the Notice of Appearance states that the company intends to resist her complaint on the following grounds:

The Response of Ran Dee Ltd:

'We intend to resist this application because we dispute the allegations that Mr Andy Handy sexually harassed the Applicant.

The Respondent carried out an internal investigation and found no substance in the allegations. The Applicant was not selected for promotion because there was another more qualified candidate who matched the job requirements.

The Respondent has a policy that it does not tolerate sexual discrimination.'

On receipt of the response, the tribunal chairman will usually carry out preparatory work, which is known as 'case management'. Case management may involve the chairman giving a list of directions in a standard written form. 'Directions' are a list of steps to be taken by the Applicant and Respondent to prepare the case for the hearing. These standard directions will probably include an order that the parties exchange and file at court an agreed bundle of documents to be used at the hearing as well as statements of the evidence to be given by any witnesses.

The tribunal may decide to hold a hearing to determine the appropriate directions. This will usually be conducted by the chairman, without the lay members, and evidence will not normally be given. At directions hearings, the chairman will do one or more of the following:

‣ identify the issues to be considered at the main hearing
‣ make orders about the information to be given or documents to be disclosed, and any other matters considered necessary for the proper preparation of the hearing
‣ determine how much time should be allocated for the hearing
‣ fix a date for the hearing

The Applicant and Respondent must advise the chairman at the directions hearing of any dates when they and their witnesses will not be available.

If it appears to the tribunal that either party's case has no reasonable prospect of success, it may arrange a 'pre-hearing review'. The tribunal will write to say whose case is going to be considered. No evidence is given and neither party is required to bring witnesses to this pre hearing review. The parties will be asked to explain the basis of their case.

If the tribunal decides that a party whose case is under consideration is unlikely to succeed, it can order the party to pay a deposit as a condition of being allowed to continue. The deposit must be paid within the time period specified otherwise the case will be struck out.

If the case continues, it will be heard by a different tribunal to the one which heard the pre-hearing review.

ACAS settlement

The tribunal office will send a copy of every IT1 to the Advisory Conciliation and Arbitration Service (ACAS) and ACAS may become involved in the case in an attempt to resolve the dispute through negotiation.

If an agreement is achieved, the details of the settlement are formalised in a document drafted by the ACAS officer, which is known as a 'COT3 Settlement' (because of the number of the form it is written on).

These COT3 agreements are binding on both parties, which means that the parties may take no further legal action against each other in respect of that particular dispute, except to take steps to enforce the agreement if its terms are not complied with.

Compromise Agreements

This is another form of settlement of a claim between employer and employee. The agreement is usually drafted by the employer's lawyer on the basis that they have more resources than the employee. A compromise agreement is a simple way of resolving disputes but a number of conditions must be satisfied for the agreement to be valid in law.

For it to be valid it must:

▶ relate to the particular dispute between the parties

▶ be in writing

▶ have been agreed by the employee, who must have received independent advice from a qualified lawyer or a competent trade union official or a competent advice centre worker

▶ identify the independent adviser in the agreement

▶ indicate that the professional adviser is insured against claims for professional negligence

▶ contain a declaration that the formalities above have been satisfied

If the conditions are satisfied, the agreement will be legally binding on both parties and will act as full and final settlement of that dispute.

In the case of Fiona Buckingham and Ran Dee Ltd, they reach an agreement to settle and the lawyers for Ran Dee Ltd draft a compromise agreement. A draft of the agreement reads as follows:

SETTLEMENT AGREEMENT:
THIS AGREEMENT dated the 2 Day of January 2004 is made between:
(1) Ran Dee Ltd of 10 Market Industrial Estate, Upmarket and
(2) Fiona Buckingham of 20 Penguin Gardens, Upmarket
WHEREAS it is agreed as follows:
1. The Employer shall, within 14 days of the date of this agreement, pay to the Employee the gross sums of
2.   a. £ X   for loss of employment;
     b. £X   for injury to feelings;
such sums being in full and final settlement of any claim aris-

ing out of her employment including her claim number XXXX but with the exception of the Employee's accrued pension rights and any claim for damages for personal injury.

3. The Employee agrees to accept the payment in full and final settlement of any claim arising out of the Employee's employment, whether under the Employment Rights Act 1996, the Sex Discrimination Act 1975, or otherwise (with the exception of the Employee's accrued pension rights and any claim for damages for personal injury).

4. The Employer will provide a reference in the terms attached to this Agreement or on no less favourable terms, to anyone seeking a reference in respect of the Employee's employment with the Employer.

5. The Employer will provide an apology to the Employee in the terms attached to this agreement.

6. The Employee acknowledges that, before entering into this agreement, she received independent legal advice from a qualified lawyer, namely Miss Ally Beal of Fish, Cage and Co who carries a policy of insurance, as to the terms and effect of this agreement and in particular as to its effect in relation to her rights to bring a claim of discrimination in the Employment Tribunal.

7. The conditions regulating compromise agreements under the Employment Rights Act 1996 and the Sex Discrimination Act 1975 are satisfied in relation to this agreement.

Signed: ....by or on behalf of the employer
Dated: ....

Signed: ....by or on behalf of the employee
Dated: ....

I, Ally Beal of Fish Cage and Co, confirm that I am a solicitor of the Supreme Court currently in possession of a practising certificate from the Law Society and that I have advised the employee as to the terms of this agreement, in particular as to its effect in relation to rights to bring claims in the Employment Tribunal.

Signed: ....
Dated: ....

Interim Applications

The employment tribunal can at any stage give directions on a matter in connection with the proceedings. Either party can make an application to the tribunal and this is done by letter as no special forms are required. The tribunal chairman may decide the matter alone and without a hearing.

In some cases, a hearing may be arranged and oral arguments presented. An example of an interim application would be where one party requests further information about the other side's case, often referred to as a request for 'further and better particulars'.

The party requesting further details should first write to the other side seeking the information by a particular date. If they refuse or delay in replying, then an application to the tribunal should be made in good time before the main hearing.

Such an application might be appropriate where, for example, the employer has merely stated that the employee was dismissed because he was 'incompetent and incapable'. The employee is entitled to have all the facts on which the employer will rely to support this contention.

An application can be made to the tribunal to strike out the applicant's complaint or the employer's reply on the following grounds:

▸ it is scandalous - it raises matters not fit to be raised in an employment tribunal

▸ it is frivolous - it is so manifestly misconceived as to have no prospect of success

▸ it is vexatious - presented without any expectation of success, but out of spite or to harass the respondent

▸ the party fails to comply with an order by the employment tribunal for further particulars of their case, fails to provide answers to written questions or discovery (*see later*)

▸ for want of prosecution

Employment tribunals are used to dealing with claims from unrepresented parties which may be not be drafted as well as if they had been done by a lawyer. Therefore, the tribunal is reluctant to exercise the power to strike out a case.

Applicants and Respondents may amend their cases at any time with permission of the employment tribunal. The tribunal freely allows amendments provided the other party is not prejudiced by the amendment.

Questionnaires

In race, sex and disability discrimination cases, the applicant may deliver to the respondent a special questionnaire which goes further than a request for further and better particulars and probes the evidence which is to be given at the tribunal. The questionnaire is available in a standard form SD74, an extract of which is set out below. Replies to the questions are admissible as evidence before the employment tribunal.

Although the tribunal has no power to compel a party to answer questions on the questionnaire, if the employer fails to reply within a reasonable time or is evasive in the replies it gives, the employment tribunal may infer, if it is just and equitable to do so, that such a failure or refusal may be evidence that the employer has committed the alleged act.

Form SD74:

Details of job

▸ *Please confirm that I was employed by (the company) from (dates) as a (job title).*

Regarding the harassment

▸ *Please state clearly and in detail which parts of paragraph 2 are admitted and which are denied.*

▸ *Do you accept that (Mr X) subjected me to the discriminatory treatment stated in part 2 of this form?*

▸ *If any of my allegations are disbelieved, please state which and give reasons.*

▸ *Did I ever give you the impression that I welcomed the treatment described in part 2 of this form?*

▸ *Please confirm that I made it clear that I did not welcome the treatment described in part 2 of this form.*

▸ *Did any member of staff report or mention to any manger the difficulties that I was experiencing with (Mr X) or notice my distress at work?*

Investigation of Complaint

▸ *When I complained of sexual harassment by Mr X on (date) what investigations did you undertake, including all meetings and interviews with dates and persons involved?*

▸ *Please give the name of every member of staff spoken to as part of the investigation, stating also:*

* *Who spoke to them and on what date(s) and time(s)*
* *Whether they were told about the allegations*
* *Who else was present, if anyone*
* *What they were asked and what was the response*
* *Whether statements were made and when. If so, please supply copies.*

▸ *Please give the name and job title of the persons involved in the investigation of my complaint.*

▸ *Please provide a copy of all procedures and guidelines for managers on the investigation of complaints of harassment and discrimination and the procedures to be followed.*

▸ *What training, if any, had the interviewing officers and investigators had in investigating complaints of harassment?*

▸ *Why did the investigation of my complaint take (number of) days/weeks/months?*

▸ *What was the outcome of the investigation and what conclusions were drawn from the outcome?*

▸ *Why was I still required to work with Mr X whilst my complaint was under investigation?*

Previous complaints

▸ *Please give details of any other complaints or allegations of sexual harassment, bullying or other similar conduct, whether formal or informal, which have been made against Mr X during his employment with (the company), including the date, the nature of the allegations, the complainant and what action, if any was taken, as a result of the complaint.*

▸ *Please give details of all grievances of any nature, whether formal or informal by any member of staff during Mr X's employment, including the date, the nature of the allegations,* the complainant and what action, if any was taken, as a result of the grievance.

▶ *Please give details of any complaints of sexual harassment or other harassment, bullying or other similar conduct at work that have been made by any employee within the last five years, including the date, the job title and location of the employee making the allegation, the name of the alleged harasser, how they were dealt with and the outcome of the complaints.*

If disciplinary hearing of alleged harasser has taken place

▶ *Please provide a copy of the contemporaneous notes and documents relating to or arising out of all disciplinary interviews/hearings of Mr X.*

▶ *Please state whether Mr X was suspended during the investigation and, if so, for what period.*

If the respondents have raised poor performance by the applicant

▶ *Was there any criticism of my conduct, attendance or performance during my employment? If so, please provide full details of each alleged incident or failing in my work giving dates and examples.*

▶ *Please state the name and job title of the person(s) who brought any criticism of my work to your attention.*

▶ *How was this criticism brought to my attention, when and by whom, and what was asked of me in the way of improvement?*

If dismissed

▶ *Please give full written reasons for my dismissal.*

▶ *Was I dismissed because I rejected (Mr X's) sexual advances?*

▶ *When and by whom (name and job title) was it decided that I should be dismissed?*

▶ *Please provide full details of my duties and responsibilities prior to my dismissal.*

▶ *Please state the name, age, sex, job title and length of service of any staff now carrying out the work previously undertaken by me.*

▶ *Please provide a copy of (or describe in full) the company's disciplinary procedure.*

▶ *Please specify which stages of the disciplinary procedure were implemented in my case.*

▶ *Please state the sex and job title of all staff dismissed in the last three years stating the reason for the dismissal and the stage of the disciplinary procedure reached at the date of dismissal.*

▶ *Why was the disciplinary procedure not followed in my case?*

Bundle of documents

Long before the hearing date, the parties should try and agree a bundle of documents to go before the employment tribunal. The fact that a party agrees that a particular document should be in the bundle does not mean that the party necessarily agrees with the contents or the use to which the document may be put; merely that it may be referred to at the hearing.

It is advisable to send a copy of the bundle to the tribunal in advance of the hearing, although not all tribunals will actually read the bundle before the hearing.

It is vital to ensure that the bundle of documents is prepared properly. A party that presents a bundle that is illegible and without numbered pages is likely to lose the sympathy of the tribunal.

Witness Statement

It is common for the tribunal to require each party to exchange witness statements and file a copy at the tribunal office before the hearing. A witness statement should set out the oral evidence which the witness, including the party themselves, will give at the hearing.

The witness statement should be set out as shown below, with each separate point being in numbered paragraphs. The witness should only set out facts as he/she perceived them and he/she should avoid giving opinion.

IN THE EMPLOYMENT TRIBUNAL
CASE No.   UPMARKET
Between:

                Fiona Buckingham   (Applicant)
        -       AND -

                Ran Dee Limited   (Respondent)

WITNESS STATEMENT OF THE APPLICANT

I Fiona Buckingham of 20 Penguin Gardens, Upmarket will say as follows:

1. I was born on the 19 December 1969 and am aged 34. I live at the above address.

2. I started working for the respondent on 10 September 1999 as a Public Relations Executive...

The Hearing

Employment tribunals are normally open to the public but there are occasions, such as where there are issues of national security, when the case will be heard in private. Either party may submit a written representation to the tribunal but must do so at least seven days before the hearing.

A party should not rely on this procedure as a written statement is bound to have less force than evidence given in the tribunal room. The tribunal may postpone a hearing but it is likely to probe the reasons for the inability to attend especially where a party initially indicated that the date or dates were suitable. If a party fails to attend the hearing, the employment tribunal may:

▶ Dismiss the case
▶ Hear the application in his/her absence or
▶ Adjourn the hearing to another date

On arriving at the hearing, both parties should seek out the tribunal clerk who will need to take a note of parties, representatives and witnesses. If an employee decides to instruct a lawyer, it should be remembered that costs are rarely awarded by the tribunal. It may be more advisable to seek the assistance of a trade union official or an advice worker from the Citizen's Advice Bureau to help present the case.

Tribunals may award costs where a party has behaved frivolously, vexatiously, abusively, disruptively or otherwise unreasonably in bringing or conducting the proceedings. Tribunals have exercised their discretion to award costs where:

▶ The employer made allegations of criminal conduct against the employee but failed to attend the hearing to substantiate them

▶ The employer's representative only gave the employee's representative a large number of documents on the morning of the hearing.

▶ The application was withdrawn on the date of the hearing

▶ The application was brought merely as a bargaining counter in relation to a claim for personal injuries

Where a party is unrepresented, the Chairman will take an active role in the proceedings. He will assist the unrepresented party by putting questions which an experienced advocate would put to witnesses. However, an unrepresented party should prepare properly for the hearing.

When the tribunal asks you to put your case it is worth having a concise opening statement of the basis of your complaint (or response). Also, it is useful to have prepared a list of questions that you want to put to your opponent's witnesses. Above all, an unrepresented party should avoid rambling on about irrelevant matters or exchanging insults with an opponent.

The decision

The tribunal may give its decision at the end of the hearing, in which case the Chairman will usually dictate it onto tape at the end of the hearing itself, or the tribunal may reserve its judgment.

In either case, a written decision will be sent to the parties in due course. The document containing the reasons for the decision must be entered in the register of decisions which is open to public inspection unless a specific order is made in the case of sexual misconduct.

The employment tribunal has no power of enforcement of its own and cannot commit anyone for breach of its orders. An order for the payment of money may be registered in the appropriate county court. Where an order for reinstatement or re-engagement is made but has been disobeyed, the only sanction is an additional award which can be enforced in the county court.

To enforce an award in the county court, you must register it in the county court for the district in which the defaulting party either resides or carries on business. This is done by an application which must:

▸ verify the amount remaining due from the defaulting party

▸ attach a copy of the relevant award, together with a court fee of £30

An Appeal

An appeal will succeed where the employment tribunal has wrongly applied a legal principle, misunderstood a statute or reached a decision which is perverse in the sense that no reasonable employment tribunal properly directed could have reached such a decision.

An appeal to the Employment Appeals Tribunal must be made within 42 days of the date on which the reasons in extended form were sent to the parties.

13.

TRADE UNIONS AND INDUSTRIAL ACTION

This chapter covers the legal aspects of trade unions and its members, the main focus being the legality of industrial action and the liability of unions.

What is a Trade Union ?

The broad definition of a trade union is contained in the Trade Union & Labour Relations (Consolidation) Act 1992 (TULRCA 1992). According to the Act it is an organisation of workers, or an association whose principal purpose includes the regulation of relations between those workers and their employers.

Under the 1992, a trade union is capable of:

‣ Making contracts in its own name
‣ Suing or being sued in its own name
‣ Having proceedings brought against it for offences committed by it or on its behalf

There is a rather curious exception to the right to sue, in that a union is not able to bring an action for defamation in its own name.

The Independence and Recognition of Trade Unions

For a trade union to enjoy full legal status, it needs to be granted independent status. To have independent status it cannot be under the control of, or liable to interference from, an employer.

A certificate of independence is issued by the Certification Officer and is conclusive evidence for all purposes that the union is independent. The current Certification Officer is Mr David Cockburn, a solicitor at Pattinson & Brewer and an expert on trade union law.

Trade unions make annual returns to the Certification Officer, who in turn makes an annual report to ACAS and the Secretary of State. The issuing of a certificate of independence is not a rubber stamp exercise. An application from News International Staff Association was recently rejected as it was thought that the employer had played a close and controlling role in the development of the organisation.

Recognition of a trade union by the relevant employer is important as it entitles the union to involvement in collective bargaining activities. An employer may choose to recognise a union voluntarily or there are procedures laid down under the Employment Relations Act 1999.

Under the 1999 Act, if the union's claim for recognition for collective bargaining purposes cannot be resolved, a union can refer the matter to the Central Arbitration Committee (CAC). The role of the CAC, which is a statutory body, is to determine the scope of the bargaining unit and to declare whether the union should be recognised on the basis that a majority of the workers supported recognition in a ballot.

The freedom of association is a fundamental principle. It is contained in Article 11 of the European Convention on Human Rights. This freedom of association includes the right to form and join trade unions.

'Closed shops' existed prior to 1988 when to gain employment in certain professions one had to belong to a trade union. The Conservative government under Margaret Thatcher introduced legislation that affected this practice.

Under the present law, an individual who loses his job, or cannot get a job, because of the closed shop agreement will be entitled to substantial compensation. A tribunal can order that the compensation be apportioned between the trade union and employer, or borne wholly by one or the other.

Until 1993, trade unions were able to specify membership qualifications so that they effectively decided who should or should not be allowed to join the union. The position changed in 1993 when individuals gained the right not to be excluded or expelled from a union except in limited situations.

Certain groups of workers are not permitted to join trade unions, such as members of the security services and the police although the police are automatically members of the Police Federation.

The rules of each union will form a contract between that union and its members. The union rules and disciplinary procedures are open to scrutiny by the courts. All union members have the right not to be unjustly disciplined by their trade union. A member who is treated in this way can present a complaint to an employment tribunal.

Industrial Action

When workers go on strike or take other forms of industrial action they will usually be in breach of their contracts of employment. This means that when trade unions or others call for or otherwise organise industrial action, they are in effect calling for a breach of or interference with contracts. A work to rule can be regarded as a breach of contract along with a refusal to work non contractual overtime.

The main statutory definition of a strike is contained in the Employment Rights Act 1996. It describes a strike as being:

> *'a cessation of work by a body of employed persons acting in combination or a concerted refusal, or a refusal under a common understanding, of any number of employed persons to continue to work for an employer in consequences of a dispute...which is done as a means of compelling their employer...to accept or not to accept terms or conditions of or affecting employment'*

There is a much shorter reference to a 'strike' in the Trade Union & Labour Relations (Consolidation) Act 1992 where it is described as 'any concerted stoppage of work'. Being on strike will have certain consequences for the employee.

The time spent on strike is not included in an employee's continuous employment, for instance. An employee dismissed while on unofficial strike usually forfeits any right to unfair dismissal compensation. However, the three month time-limit for presenting a complaint for unfair dismissal is doubled to six months if the employee was on strike when he was dismissed.

Statutory Immunities

Without special protection, known as statutory immunities, the trade union could face legal action for inducing a breach of contract every time it called a strike. These immunities have the effect that trade unions and individuals can in certain circumstances organise industrial action without fear of being sued in the courts. They grant protection to those who call for, threaten to call, or otherwise organise industrial action.

The immunities are subject to a number of restrictions. When a trade union or individual calls for industrial action, there are a number of criteria that must be met to ensure there is statutory immunity from legal action. The criteria are:

- It must be a trade dispute and the strike action is called wholly or mainly in contemplation or furtherance of that dispute
- A properly conducted secret ballot must be held
- Following the ballot, notice of official industrial action must be given to employers likely to be affected by such action
- The action cannot be 'secondary' action
- The action must not be intended to promote union closed shop practices or to prevent employers using non-union firms as suppliers
- The action must not be in support of any employee dismissed while taking unofficial industrial action
- The action must not involve unlawful picketing

What is a trade dispute?

A trade dispute is a dispute between workers and their own employers wholly or mainly about employment related matters, such as pay and conditions, jobs, allocation of work, discipline, negotiating machinery and trade union membership. It would not include a dispute between groups of workers or unions where no employer is involved or between workers and an employer other than their own.

ZB Parcel Services

ZB Parcels is a world wide courier service with depots throughout the UK. A depot in Birmingham handles all the parcels and other mail that is to be taken to African countries, including Zimbabwe.

The Union calls for industrial action at the Birmingham depot because the ZB insists that the employees handle parcels bound for Zimbabwe. The Union calls a ballot and 90% of those entitled to vote support the call strike action.

If industrial action is taken by employees of ZB Parcels Services, it is likely that it would not come within the definition of a trade dispute. In various cases, the courts have decided that a 'trade dispute' does not include disputes which are motivated by political considerations.

It could be argued that the ZB dispute has political considerations, as was the case in Gouriet v. UPOW (1978) where there was a refusal to handle mail for South Africa as an anti-apartheid protest.

Secret Ballots

If a trade union decides to call for industrial action, it will have no immunity unless it first holds a properly conducted secret ballot. Before the Conservative Government trade union reforms of the 1980's, there were often examples in the media of groups of workers meeting outside and voting for industrial action by a show of hands. The law now pre-scribes certain requirements which must be complied with in relation to such a ballot. The main requirements are:

- ▾ Where more than 50 members are entitled to vote, the union must appoint a scrutineer of the ballot
- ▾ Notice of the ballot and sample voting paper for employers must be provided
- ▾ The industrial action to which the ballot relates must start within four weeks. This can be extended to eight weeks if the union and employer agree
- ▾ All those whom it is reasonable to believe at the time of the ballot will be called upon to take part in the industrial action must be given the opportunity to vote

Official or Unofficial Action?

It is important to distinguish between official and unofficial action. Official action is action supported by the trade union. In calling for the industrial action if the union has complied with the requirements gov-erning the organisation of industrial action then the action will be lawful and will be 'protected'.

By protected, it means that the action will have immunity from legal action. If the union repudiates the industrial action, it ceases to be pro-tected from legal action on the second working day after it does so. Thus if industrial action is repudiated on the Monday, then industrial action on or after Wednesday will be unofficial.

Dismissal for participation in lawful official action is automatically unfair. This protection lasts for eight weeks from the start of the official action. An employee dismissed while taking part in unofficial action will not generally be able to claim unfair dismissal.

There are situations where an employee could claim unfair dismissal where he is involved in unofficial action, such as where the reason for dismissal relates to family reasons, health and safety, employee representation and whistle blowing.

Red Robbo and Rackman Property Lettings Ltd

Rackman Property Lettings is a large private company involved in the letting and management of residential properties. "Red Robbo", as he is known by his colleagues in the lettings department, discovers what he genuinely believes are issues of health and safety.

There is no health and safety representative in the company but his role as a property manager requires him to undertake inspections of the properties.

In a number of properties, he feels he has detected serious structural faults and he reports this to his manager who tells him that the properties are fine. Red, a qualified surveyor, is adamant that there is imminent danger to the tenants in several properties.

He speaks to the union representative voicing his concerns over health and safety. The union supports a call for industrial action. The union representative organises a ballot of the 25 members in the company but by a vote of 19 to 6, union members decide not to take strike action.

Despite the vote, Red and the other five take strike action. Rackman dismiss Red claiming he is engaging in unlawful strike action. The Health and Safety Executive were told by Red of his concerns about four properties. They inspected the four properties and found a serious structural defect in one property which had not yet been let.

In the case of Red Robbo, he could have a claim for unfair dismissal despite the fact that he was engaging in unlawful strike action. He could argue that the reason for his dismissal was related to his bringing to the company's attention the concerns about health and safety issues.

It could also be said that he used reasonable means to raise the matter in view of there being no health and safety representative in the company.

Picketing

Many people have seen images in the media of the type of picketing that took place before the trade union reforms of the 1980's. The term 'flying picket' came to prominence during the miners strike of 1984. Striking miners were seen travelling to areas of work other than their own.

Under section 220 of the TULR(C)A 1992, it is lawful for a person in furtherance of a trade dispute to attend:

(a) at or near his own place of work , or

(b) if he is an official of a trade union, at or near the place of work of the member of the union whom he is accompanying and whom he represents, for the purpose only of peacefully obtaining information, or peacefully persuading any person to work or abstain from working.

For picketing to be lawful, it must take place at or near the pickets' workplace. If your workplace is in London but you travel to Birmingham to picket outside that branch of your employer, the picketing may not be lawful. The picketing must also be peaceful.

The courts have decided that a large number of pickets might not be regarded as 'peacefully communicating', their purpose being to intimidate. In a case arising out of the miners strike in 1985, a court restricted the number of pickets to 6, because the large picket was designed to intimidate and not peacefully communicate or persuade.

Employer's Remedies Against Individual Employees

An employer may be able to sue an employee for his/her involvement in strike action. However, the courts will not grant the remedy of specific performance against an individual i.e. they will not physically order an employee to do something. Damages may be awarded but only for the individual's own contribution to the loss and so such a remedy is rarely sought in practice.

Section 14(5) of the Employment Rights Act 1996 permits deductions from wages on account of the worker having taken part in a strike or other industrial action.

SPECIMEN FORMS

Application to an Employment Tribunal

For office use

Received at ET

- If you fax this form you do not need to send one in the post.
- This form has to be photocopied. Please use CAPITALS and black ink (if possible).
- Where there are tick boxes, please tick the one that applies.

Case number

Code

Initials

---

1 Please give the type of complaint you want the tribunal to decide (for example, unfair dismissal, equal pay). A full list is available from the tribunal office. If you have more than one complaint list them all.

2 Please give your details

Mr ☐ Mrs ☐ Miss ☐ Ms ☐ Other _____

First names

Surname

Date of birth

Address

Postcode

Phone number

Daytime phone number

Please give an address to which we should send documents if different from above

Postcode

3 If a representative is acting for you please give details (all correspondence will be sent to your representative)

Name

Address

Postcode

Phone | Fax

Reference

---

4 Please give the dates of your employment

From | to

5 Please give the name and address of the employer, other organisation or person against whom this complaint is being brought

Name

Address

Postcode

Phone number

Please give the place where you worked or applied to work if different from above

Address

Postcode

6 Please say what job you did for the employer (or what job you applied for). If this does not apply, please say what your connection was with the employer

---

116

7 Please give the number of normal basic hours worked each week

Hours per week

9 If your complaint is not about dismissal, please give the date when the matter you are complaining about took place

8 Please give your earning details

Basic wage or salary

£   per

Average take home pay

£   per

Other bonuses or benefits

£   per

10 Unfair dismissal applicants only

Please indicate what you are seeking at this stage, if you win your case

☐ Reinstatement: to carry on working in your old job as before (an order for reinstatement normally includes an award of compensation for loss of earnings).

☐ Re-engagement: to start another job or new contract with your old employer (an order for re-engagement normally includes an award of compensation for loss of earnings).

☐ Compensation only: to get an award of money

11 Please give details of your complaint

If there is not enough space for your answer, please continue on a separate sheet and attach it to this form.

12 Please sign and date this form, then send it to the address on the back page of this booklet.

Signed   Date

EMPLOYMENT TRIBUNALS

NOTICE OF APPEARANCE BY RESPONDENT

In the application of

Case Number
(please quote in all correspondence)

* This form has to be photocopied, if possible use Black Ink and Capital letters
* If there is not enough space for your answer, please continue on a separate sheet and attach it to this form

1. Full name and address of the Respondent:	3. Do you intend to resist the application? (Tick appropriate box)

YES   NO

☐   ☐

4. Was the applicant dismissed? (Tick appropriate box)
YES   NO

☐   ☐

Please give
reason below

Reason for dismissal:

5. Are the dates of employment given by the applicant correct? (Tick appropriate box)

Postcode:

YES   NO

Telephone number:

☐   ☐

please give correct dates

2. If you require documents and notices to be sent to a representative or any other address in the United Kingdom please give details:

Began on

Ended on

6. Are the details given by the applicant about wages/salary, take home or other bonuses correct? (Tick appropriate box)
YES   NO

☐   ☐

Please give correct details
below

Basic Wages/Salary	£	per
Average take Home Pay	£	per
Other bonuses/Benefits	£	per

PLEASE TURN OVER

Postcode:

For office use only
Date of receipt   Initials

Reference:

Telephone number:

7. Give particulars of the grounds on which you intend to resist the application.

8. Please sign and date the form.

Signed   Dated

DATA PROTECTION ACT 1984
We may put some of the information you give on this form to a computer. This helps us to monitor progress and produce statistics. We may also give information to:
* the other party in the case
* other parts of the DTI and organisations such as ACAS (Advisory Conciliation and Arbitration Service), the Equal Opportunities Commission or the Commission for Racial Equality.

Please post or fax this form to:

* IF YOU FAX THE FORM, DO NOT POST A COPY AS WELL
* IF YOU POST THE FORM, TAKE A COPY FOR YOUR RECORDS

If you have found this book useful you may also find other books by Fitzwarren Handbooks of interest.

The E-Commerce Handbook
Andrew Sparrow
A practical legal guide to doing business over the internet, including suggested terms and conditions, use of domain names and trademarks, website development contracts, advertising agreements etc.

The Landlord & Tenants Handbook
Robert Kay
A practical guide to renting property, looking at the potential pitfalls from both the landlords' and tenants' point of view.

The Litigation Handbook
Anthony Reeves and Alan Matthews
A concise account of how the English civil courts operate. Contains valuable information to enable the reader to pursue - or defend - a simple claim in the county court.

The Elections Handbook
Ron Kendall
An in-depth account of UK election procedures. An invaluable guide for electoral staff or for anyone running for public office.

Fitzwarren Handbooks provide helpful jargon-free guidance on a number of legal subjects. Written by professionals but with the layman in mind, the books are presented in a clear, easy-to-read style invaluable to lay persons and yet with sufficient depth to be of assistance to lawyers and other professionals working in relevant areas.